The Roehampton Teaching Studies Series

This new series of books is aimed primarily at student and practising teachers. It covers key issues in current educational debate relating to age phases, school management, the curriculum and teaching methods. Each volume examines the topic critically, bringing out the practical implications for teachers and school organisation.

Authors – not necessarily based at Roehampton – are commissioned by an Editorial Board at the Roehampton Institute, one of the United Kingdom's leading centres of educational research as well as undergraduate and postgraduate training.

The General Editor of the series is Dr Jim Docking, formerly Chairman of the Institute's School of Education.

A selection of recent and forthcoming titles appears on the back cover of this book.

WORSHIP IN THE PRIMARY SCHOOL

Elaine McCreery

David Fulton Publishers

London

Published in association with the Roehampton Institute

David Fulton Publishers Ltd
2 Barbon Close, London WC1N 3JX

First published in Great Britain by
David Fulton Publishers 1993

Note: the right of the author to be identified as the author of this work has been
asserted by her in accordance with the Copyright, Designs and Patents Act 1988.

Copyright © Elaine McCreery

British Library Cataloguing in Publication Data

A catalogue record for this book is available from the British Library

ISBN 1-85346-233-0

Typeset by Witwell Ltd, Southport
Printed in Great Britain by BPCC Journals, Exeter.

Contents

Dedication

This book is dedicated to Jacqueline and George McCreery – for reasons they already know.

Introduction

The subject of worship in school is one which has caused much controversy and debate over the years. It has been a compulsory part of children's education in this country since 1944, yet in spite of this, or because of it, there remains much confusion and nervousness about its rightful place in schools. This book is an attempt to address some of the issues surrounding the subject and offer teachers a way forward.

In 1991, as part of some research work, I made a study of three primary schools and their approach to worship. I was particularly interested to discover how they had responded to the terms of the 1988 Education Reform Act and its provisions for worship. I knew that for many teachers the issue of worship presented a problem and that feelings of unease surrounded the purpose and value of the activity (see, for example, Copley, 1989). With the advent of the new legislation, which confirmed the place of worship in school, I wanted to know how schools were implementing the terms, and if the Act heralded a revived interest in the subject.

What I found was that the schools were struggling, both to understand the terms of the Act and to translate it in a practical way which provided a meaningful and educational activity for their children. Coupled with this was the added pressure of the many recent changes in primary education, particularly regarding the National Curriculum. Understandably, teachers did not appear to have the time nor the inclination to embark on a detailed examination of the Act or what it meant for them.

Since the Act, a variety of publications have appeared which offer help to schools. Apart from the DES Circular 3/89, local education authorities have produced guidelines to help schools pick their way through the Act, and find ways of incorporating the terms into their provision. Alongside these there have been several recent publications which aim to assist teachers when planning assemblies. This book is an attempt to bring these two types of literature together, addressing both the theoretical framework for worship and the practical implications. It is based on the belief that before assemblies can be planned, there must be a clear understanding of what the activity is for, and of how staff and children can contribute to worship without compromising their own beliefs and values.

The book begins by establishing why it is that worship is a compulsory part of the curriculum by reviewing its history in school. It goes on to explain the terms of the 1988 Act and offers some ways of understanding it by reference to recent material. Subsequent chapters explore the purpose, planning, organisation and presentation of worship and these are followed by particular reference to the needs of both infant and junior children. The opportunities for incorporating worship into aspects of the National Curriculum are also explored. The book concludes with a consideration of how schools might work towards a whole-school policy for worship, and this is recommended as a positive way forward.

The book is aimed primarily at those teachers, mainly in non-religious schools, who are new to collective worship. This includes not only those new to teaching, but also those teachers who may be unfamiliar with the Act or the role of worship and also those who may be returning to teaching. These groups have been foremost in my mind during the writing of the book. As a result, I am aware that there are issues concerning worship which merit further consideration and are not as simple as they appear here. This is because the intention has been to offer positive, constructive suggestions for practising teachers. Those who are interested in exploring the issue of school worship further are recommended to read some of the books listed in the bibliography.

While the main audience for the book is teachers, there is no doubt that it may be of use to anyone involved in the education of children, particularly governors and parents who are concerned about the role worship plays in the life of the school.

The book is written with the conviction that worship should be a rewarding, stimulating, educational part of the school day, and that it offers an ideal opportunity to focus explicitly on those areas of human experience such as beliefs, values, feelings and aspirations, which are vital to the healthy development of our children.

CHAPTER 1
The History and Development of Collective Worship

Introduction

In 1988 the Education Reform Act was passed which made significant changes in the education of young people. It brought in a whole new approach to the curriculum and introduced the idea of national assessment. Four sections outlined provision for religious education and collective worship. These two areas were considered to be distinct from the rest of the curriculum and for this reason were not to be included in the National Curriculum or assessment. However, the clauses which referred to religious education and worship became the focal point of a great deal of discussion and argument as various groups attempted to understand the legislation. Those on collective worship were subject to particular scrutiny. The debate continues to the present day.

What is this subject 'collective worship' and why did it cause such debate? The answers are deeply embedded in the history of English education dating back to a time long before any Government took an interest in the education of children. Worship has had a place on the school timetable from the earliest days of church school education. When county schools were established, they too included it on the timetable and since 1944 it has been compulsory for schools to provide it. In no other western country is collective worship required by law in school. Indeed in many countries it would be illegal to include it. But in England and Wales worship remains and continues to invite debate and criticism from many quarters.

This chapter is an attempt to explain the phenomenon of collective worship, and seeks to explore how the activity became a lasting feature of school life. It will describe the changing face of collective worship over the years, influenced by changes in legislation and attitudes, and ultimately it will explain why, by 1988, there was the desire to bring in new legislation governing collective worship.

The history and development of collective worship has been characterised in two ways. Firstly, there has been legislation which defined its nature and stipulated how it should be executed. Secondly, there has been, as Souper and Kay (1982) describe it, 'the "public" debate which has taken place in the press and academic journals' (pii). In many ways the legislation and the debate are inextricably linked in that one often informs the other, as will be made apparent in the sections which follow.

The origins of collective worship

The origins of collective worship in school arise from the fact that from early times England was a Christian country. As Tilby (1979) says, 'England was part of Christendom, and Christendom meant that the church saw it as her task to "Christianize" culture' (p24). The power of the church was strengthened by the fact that the head of state was also head of the church. The earliest schools were those attached to churches and cathedrals. Tilby also notes that until 1650 all schoolmasters and university teachers had to be ordained clergy.

During the eighteenth and early nineteenth centuries charity schools began to emerge to provide for the education of poor children. Until then education had been the preserve of the wealthy classes. Among these church initiatives, the Sunday School Movement, from the 1780s, offered teaching in reading and writing along with religious instruction. Such instruction tended to consist of rote learning of the basics of Christian doctrine. Elementary schools set up by the British and Foreign School Society (founded in 1808 for the children of non-conformists), the National Society (founded in 1811 for 'promoting the education of the poor in the principles of the Established Church'), and the Catholic Poor Schools Committee (founded in 1847) offered a similar curriculum. It is important to note that in these earliest days there was no distinction between 'religious education' and 'worship'; the one prepared children for participation in the other. 'Religious observances' as they were called usually took place every day (Hull, 1975).

The 1870 Elementary Education Act

Despite successes in the development of elementary education, it was clear that religious organisations were unable to provide schooling for more than a minority of the nation's children. There was, however, division among the churches about the state moving into the field, and many felt that schooling should be left to voluntary organisations, with the state giving grants to the charities.

The Education Act of 1870 involved the state more directly. In order to provide education in the gaps left by the churches, the Act provided for local school boards to set up schools in districts where adequate provision was not already made. The board schools were open to all children and were non-denominational. When it came to religious instruction, there was never any doubt that it should be part of children's education, but it too was to be non-denominational. This marked the beginning of a new type of religious education and worship, one that was essentially Christian but did not reflect any particular denomination. The Cowper Temple Clause of the 1870 Act ensured that this was the case. It stated that 'No religious Catechism or religious formulary which is distinctive of any particular denomination shall be taught in any school provided by a school board', and parents could insist that their children did not attend religious education or worship. This was the start of what Tilby (1979) refers to as the 'beginning of the secularization of religious education' (p27), ending the system whereby no school was entitled to public funding unless it was connected with one of the religious societies.

For the first time religious instruction could be taught by teachers who were not clergy. However, the Act also marked the beginning of a confusion in religious education which has remained to the present day. In the church schools, religious instruction was clearly intended to make children Christians. What was its purpose in the board schools? Some of these schools dropped religious instruction altogether, while others concentrated on the Bible stories and rote learning of the Creed and prayers. Circulars to school boards produced by the Government during the late 1870s showed that the majority of schools included religious observances as part of their daily life (Hull, 1975, p12).

The dual system

The 1902 Education Act transferred educational administration from the school boards to local authorities. They took responsibility for secular education in the voluntary (religious) schools as well as the running of county (non-religious) schools, whilst the churches maintained control of RE and worship in church schools. These local authorities began to draw up 'Agreed Syllabuses' which outlined appropriate religious instruction for the county schools. This dual system, whereby education was provided by both church and state, continues to the present day.

4

The Agreed Syllabuses, which began to appear during the 1900s, were so called because they represented agreement by various parties on what should be taught. The conferences set up to decide on the syllabus consisted of representatives from the Church of England, the local authority, teachers and other denominations represented in the area. Such syllabuses required the inclusion of worship in the school day, as the culmination of the work of the school. County and voluntary schools alike were seen as Christian communities, in which assembly played a special role:

> The school affirmed explicitly what was implicit in all of its work, namely its aspiration towards divine society of which it was the image. The school would lift its heart in worship of God. (Hull, 1975, p24)

The 1944 Butler Education Act

The 1944 Act, which restructured the whole education system, must be seen in the light of world events. Coming as it did during the Second World War, it sought to bring about a new era of stability in the lives of the nation and its children. The evils perpetrated by the extremes of facism had devastated society, and the clauses on religious instruction and worship were intended to strengthen Christian values. The provisions reflected the practice of many schools which included worship as a daily part of the curriculum.

The Act now made a daily act of worship compulsory for the first time. Schools were to start the day worshipping God. The prerogative of parents to withdraw their children from worship had been in place since 1870, and the new Act re-affirmed this right, together with similar protection for teachers. The Act also reflected a new distinction between religious education and collective worship. The activities were now distinct and both had to be a regular feature of school life.

The 1944 Act did not describe the content or form of school worship (except in stipulating that in county schools it was to be non-denominational), but parliament clearly saw it as part of the Christian education of the nation's children. The provisions remained in place until the Education Reform Act of 1988. Such legislation is peculiar to English education in that no other western country requires it by law. Due to the lack of guidance concerning the nature of school worship, developments over the years produced a variety of forms. That confusion and misunderstanding abounded is not surprising when one considers that: 'It is only in England that the law requires religious education to be evangelical, but not church based, linked to formal worship, but worship of no known denomination or sect' (Tilby, 1979, p43).

The 1944 Act permitted local authorities to establish Standing Advisory Councils on Religiouis Education, usually referred to as 'SACREs', which were intended to assist in the provision of religious education and worship (Education Act 1944, section 29, 2). The constitution of these was left to the decision of the local authorities, and they were often made up of similar groups to those on Agreed Syllabus conferences. Their role was not always clear, but many provided a useful body which could advise and take an interest in developments in RE and worship. Not all local authorities established such a council and their sphere of influence and power was not always evident.

Developments in worship 1944–88

In the absence of further legislation on school worship during the next four decades, many writers have attempted to make sense of the subject in the light of changes in society, attitudes and values. Although thinking about worship developed and expanded, confusion was such that, in 1975, John Hull called his book *School Worship – An Obituary*. Tracing the history of worship from its earliest days, Hull concluded that the old model of worship as understood by the 1944 Act was an out-dated activity. He argued that a new way of thinking about worship was necessary if it was to have any role in the schools of the future. What had happened to worship in the years since 1944?

Slee (1990) notes that during the 1950s and 1960s school worship continued to 'support the concept and practice of school worship as an explicitly religious act, by and large' (p6). She adds that the Plowden Committee in 1967 recognised the value of assemblies in unifying the school. However, by this time it was recognised that there were difficulties with the activity, especially in multi-racial schools.

The Durham Report of 1970 recognised that many schools tended to use the term 'assembly' to describe the act of worship. This indicated a change in attitude towards the activity; that teachers felt more comfortable with a term that had no particular religious connotations. Even so, the Durham report still found that, 'Assembly consists of a hymn; a reading from the Bible, or from some inspirational literature; prayers and the Lord's Prayer' (p130). It went on to argue the case for and against collective worship, concluding that worship should be retained and should be Christian in character, but that provision should be made in schools with mixed pupil population to cater for the other religions represented.

Changing attitudes towards worship can be seen in teachers' books of the period. Jean Holm, writing in 1975, said, 'The study of worship is a highly important part of religious education, but a regular act of worship is not an appropriate activity in the community's schools' (p114).

Edwin Cox, in 1983, devoted only two pages to school worship in his book on religious education. He said:

> Some modifications of the existing situation seems needed. Many religious education teachers would welcome a distinction between religious education and worship, and would like to see the legal provisions for the latter repealed, because the implication of the existing law is that teaching is intended to be confessional. (p112)

There are several reasons for the changes in attitude towards worship. Firstly it was becoming clear that in many schools there were large groups of children who were obviously not Christian and that to compel them to worship in a Christian way was unacceptable. Secondly there was the feeling that as the very nature of worship is as a voluntary activity, to demand that children participate is a contradiction. Thirdly some, like Holm, argued that what went on in school was a poor reflection of the true nature of worship within a faith community. Such worship could only give a distorted picture of corporate worship outside school, and was therefore counterproductive. Finally, it could be said that compulsory collective worship contradicts the educational aims of western schooling. Hull (1975) analyses the nature of education and worship and finds them to be incompatible. He argues that while worship assumes belief, education scrutinises belief. Because of this, collective worship is open to the charge of indoctrination and undermines the autonomy of the pupils.

How then did schools deal with these complex issues and remain within the boundaries of the law? Answers can be found in the interpretation of the term worship. From 1944, worship in schools was seen as something distinct from church worship. The term 'collective' identified it as such, with worship in county schools being non-denominational. Over the years, there developed two distinct understandings and uses of the term 'worship'. Slee (1989) describes the distinction between the two interpretations:

> On the one hand, 'worship' is understood by some as an explicitly religious concept and activity, which presupposes a foundation of religious belief and commitment, if not on the part of the individual taking part, then at least on the part of the institution which engages in the activity of worship. On the other

hand, 'worship', is understood by others in the much wider sense of 'worth-ship', the celebration and veneration of shared values, the response to what is seen to be of ultimate concern. (p5)

Many schools found that this second, less explicit interpretation offered the flexibility to stay within the law and yet provide appropriate activities for their children without compromising anyone's beliefs. Such an interpretation allowed for assemblies to be based on those values which were common to all members of the school community. Assemblies such as those based on caring for others, personal responsibility, acceptable behaviour, would fit into this idea of 'worth-ship'.

By the mid-1980s various patterns of school worship could be identified around the country. Derek Webster (1990) identified five models of collective worship which were prevalent in schools:

- *The Traditional Christian Model.* This, he says, is found only in independent, Public and church schools. It is considered part of the nurturing aspect of school life. Belief in God and commitment to the faith is assumed;
- *The Modified Christian Model* is different from the first in both form and content. An attempt to make school worship more accessible to the young, it incorporates a variety of presentations, e.g. drama and music. Christian beliefs are still assumed, however;
- *The Interfaith Model* recognises the variety of religious backgrounds of the worshippers. It attempts to bring together religious traditions to deepen tolerance and understanding;
- *The Secularised Model* represents a change in emphasis from the divine to the human. The lives of the school, the community and the world are the focal point. Webster notes the danger in this model of including trivia in the activity, e.g. football results;
- *The Other Faiths Models.* These are acts of assembly which are based on religions other than Christianity.

Webster emphasises that there needs to be clear understanding of the nature of school assembly so that neither the law nor the philosophy of the school is compromised.

Those who began to draw up the terms of the 1988 Education Reform Act were well aware of these changes in the practice of collective worship, and there were a great many who felt that the 1944 Act was well overdue for change. What those changes should be was less clear.

What was evident, however, was that many schools were regularly breaking the terms of the Act. In some, worship had disappeared from the timetable altogether, while in others it was provided only patchily, perhaps once or twice a week. Some schools were providing a pattern of worship similar to one of those outlined by Webster, while others used assembly time merely to give out notices or instructions.

The attempt to update the requirements of the 1944 Act was to be a lengthy and arduous process, complicated by the fact that there was a range of views about the whole place of worship within schools. The resulting Act in 1988 was inevitably going to be a compromise and when it emerged it started a whole new lengthy debate which continues to the present day.

The next chapter will outline the main provisions of this Act and will summarise the discussion which it has generated since.

CHAPTER 2
The 1988 Education Reform Act and Beyond

Background to the Act

The 1944 Education Act made collective worship in school compulsory for the first time. Most schools practised some form of collective worship anyway and so the Act did not bring any significant problems. There were conscience clauses built into the Act which allowed parents to withdraw their children and allowed teachers to be exempt from participating in worship. Implicit within the spirit of the law was a desire to strengthen moral and Christian values so that children would grow up to be active and responsible Christians. Slee (1990) comments that worship:

> entailed the transmission of basic Christian doctrines and beliefs, but it was widely understood to mean more than this, and to be concerned with initiating pupils into Christian faith and creating Christian community within the school. (p6)

Among those who were drafting the 1988 Education Reform Bill were many who felt that the original vision of the 1944 Act had been lost. Some critics maintained that many schools were avoiding the whole issue of worship altogether, using assembly mainly for social purposes and as a time to give out notices or team results. Other critics pointed to schools which had not ignored worship but had tried to move with the times by adopting a multi-faith approach to reflect the various backgrounds of the pupils. These critics argued that, in trying to do justice to all faiths, the schools were doing justice to none. The term 'mish-mash' was used to describe school worship of this kind.

Many commentators also pointed to the relationship between schools and what they saw as an increasingly secularised society. On the one hand there were those who regretted the way in which secular society was undermining the value of worship in schools. On the other hand there were those who argued that worship in schools had no place in secular Britain today. Far from regretting the decline of traditional forms of school worship, these critics wanted the complete removal of worship from the school timetable.

In spite of these arguments, there was evidence that many parents and other adults felt that school worship was 'a good thing' to have in schools (Copley, 1989, p13). It was recognised as a way in which children could learn about their Christian heritage, especially if they did not attend church with their family. Many Christians, though, were critical of this attitude which removed the responsibility of parents for the Christian nurture of their own children. Added to this is the historical link between the church and education, dating back for generations and seen in teacher training institutions among other places. These traditions all indicated that in some way, worship and education were compatable and desirable.

In the early stages of the 1988 Education Reform Bill there was only scant reference to worship in schools, and this was contained in a 'Miscellaneous' chapter far removed from the clauses on religious education. When this came before the House of Lords it began a series of discussions and arguments centring on the inclusion of the word 'Christian'. Some felt the word needed to be included, while others were aware of the dangers this provoked.

If we examine *Hansard* at the time of the religious education debates, we see the concern of some people in the Lords about the declining importance of school worship. There was the feeling that the state has a responsibility to provide Christian worship in schools. As Baronness Cox said:

> As a Christian nation we have a gospel to proclaim and a duty to proclaim it to our children; we have been guilty of failing to do so, and now we have an opportunity to correct that failure. (16th May, p12)

There is also clear criticism of the way in which worship had developed in schools. Lord Thorneycroft said:

> Here are these Christian children; give them at least that, an act of collective Christian worship, with rights to the others to have their religions but not all put together in some meaningless contrivance. (12th May, p1350)

Here was a direct criticism of the multi-faith type worship which had enabled many schools to make it appropriate for their pupils.

What emerged was very much a compromise which ultimately did not reconcile the differences in standpoints between the opposing groups. The Bishop of London, whose job it had been to find appropriate wording for the Bill, introduced the package by saying that he hoped it would ensure that worship was seen as an important part of school life, giving importance to Christianity, but neither imposing inappropriate forms of worship on children nor dividing schools into separate faith groups.

As details of the discussion began to emerge, great fear was spread, encouraged by media hype which warned of predominantly Christian worship for all children. The result was an Act which John Hull describes as 'undoubtedly the most obscure and complicated piece of Religious Education legislation in the history of this country' (1989b, p10). Since it was published, many writers with different perspectives have examined the Act to find out what it says, what it means and how it translates into practice in schools. In the next section there is a summary of the main points of the Act together with an attempt to interpret the requirements for school use.

What does the Act say?

A good way to examine the terms of the Act is to look at the DES commentary (Circular 3/89). This document sets out the terms by comparing them to the 1944 Act. Firstly it states those parts of the Act which are *preserved*:

- There must be a daily act of collective worship for all pupils which in county (non-church) schools must be non-denominational.
- Parents must be allowed to withdraw their children from school worship.
- Teachers are free to exempt themselves from worship.

Secondly the Circular outlines the *changes* that the Act has made:

- Collective worship can now be organised for separate school groups.
- Collective worship can be held at any time during the school day.
- The content of worship must now be 'wholly or mainly of a broadly Christian character'.
- Acts of worship must take into account the family backgrounds, ages and aptitudes of the pupils involved.

If a head teacher feels that, having taken these things into account, broadly Christian worship is not appropriate, then he or she can apply to the Standing Advisory Council on Religious Education (SACRE) for a determination that some or all of the pupils should be exempt from that type of worship. SACREs have been a feature of local authority religious education since 1944 when their principal role was to supervise the development of Agreed Syllabuses on religious education. In the 1988 Act their role is extended, and they are to act as 'watchdogs' in the absence of government guidelines in this area. Their main work is twofold:

- They may require a local authority to set up a conference to review the Agreed Syllabus.
- They will consider applications from head teachers for exemption from broadly Christian worship.

Some SACREs have begun to publish guidelines for schools on collective worship e.g. Wandsworth SACRE (1990).

There are further provisions in the Act for those parents who wish to withdraw their children from worship. Parents may arrange for their children to receive worship elsewhere, provided that:

- the child could not reasonably attend a school of the appropriate faith or denomination;
- suitable arrangements have been made;
- the local education authority is satisfied that the child will only be withdrawn at the beginning or end of the school day.

If this is difficult, the schools may, upon request, make facilities available within the school, provided that:

- it does not take the place of the non-denominational school worship;
- it does not put the school to any additional expense;
- it is consistent with the overall purpose of the school curriculum.

When the terms of the Act first emerged there was great consternation about the implications for schools. Many were concerned that the valuable patterns they had developed for worship were no longer legal. Others felt that the Act was vague and open to a variety of interpretations. A study of the provisions reveals that indeed it is open to interpretation. In order to find a way through it we must examine the provisions to see how they can be interpreted and to see how this affects what we do in school.

The Act is concerned with two aspects of worship. One is *organisation*, the other is *content*.

The organisation of worship

The aspect of the Act which deals with organisation has caused the least controversy and has indeed been welcomed by schools. It represents a relaxation of the 1944 Act and aims to make it easier for schools to assemble for worship. Collective worship must still take place every day and this presents a problem for schools who are faced with ever increasing demands on time. There has been much discussion on the validity of having worship every day, especially when most faith communities do not even demand this of their adherents.

The 1944 Act stipulated that the school day began with an act of worship. Now, under the 1988 Act, it can take place at any time during the day. This flexibility allows for worship to be timetabled at the most appropriate time for the school. The beginning of the school day is often taken up with registers, dinner money, late comers and so on. Schools therefore often find that assembling before lunch or at the end of the school day is more beneficial. However, although the timing of worship is flexible, the place is not. The Act does insist that worship takes place on the school premises. This clearly identifies the activity as a school one rather than a denominational one. If worship took place in a church there would be the danger of contravening that part of the Act which demands that worship is non-denominational. The Act also suggests that worship in schools is of a different character than that in faith communities and the emphasis on its educational value is retained. John Hull is keen to demonstrate this educational side of school worship. He says, 'To put this worship in a religious building, a building set aside for religious worship, would fundamentally change the nature of the assembly' (1989b, p119).

The 1944 Act called for a 'single' act of worship in which all the pupils of the school were present. In many schools, particularly large ones, this was impractical. Many lacked the space to assemble all their pupils, and, even if they did have the space, the time and effort required to gather everyone would far outweigh the time spent actually worshipping. The new Act gets over this problem by stating that while schools can still gather as one group, it is also permitted for assemblies to be organised for smaller groups. Pupils of different ages can meet for worship. Again schools welcome this as it enables them to assemble groups easily and content can be matched to age ranges.

In a recent study (McCreery, 1991) of how schools had responded to the 1988 Act, it was found that planning assemblies for year groups had improved provision. One head teacher felt that not only did it enable staff to pitch the assemblies at the right level but it also helped staff to feel more comfortable with the occasion. He said, 'Having the smaller more intimate assemblies has been more popular with staff and is also less threatening for those leading the assembly.' Another head said that some assemblies were held in the classroom just for that group of children.

The Act makes it clear that schools are not allowed to group children according to religion (although parents may request that alternative acts of worship are provided for children who are withdrawn from the main assembly). Some schools may have felt that this would have answered the problem of providing worship for children of different religious traditions, but as Cox and Cairns (1989) say, 'It would not be in the spirit of the Act to arrange for pupils of each religious belief to assemble for the sort of worship to which they are accustomed outside school' (p34).

The content and nature of worship

It is the aspect of the Act which deals with the content and nature of worship, which has caused the most controversy. Whereas the practical aspects appeared to have relaxed the requirements of the 1944 Act, these appear to many to have made the law more rigid. There are three phrases which have been highlighted as being both obscure and controversial. These are 'collective worship', 'wholly or mainly' and 'broadly Christian'. We will examine the meaning and implications of each.

Collective worship

This term is used almost exclusively to describe worship in schools. It is often contrasted with the term 'corporate worship' which is seen to take place within faith communities.

What does the Act mean when it talks of 'worship' in schools? There are many, including members of faith groups, who would argue that worship has no place in the education of children in state schools. They would say that it presumes a belief which may not be there, that it can implant confusing ideas in the minds of young children and that it causes problems in multi-faith schools. Further, it is said that worship goes against all traditions of the philosophy behind the British education system. The British Council of Churches says:

> Education seeks to prepare children to question, scrutinise and evaluate. Worship on the other hand, assumes the truth of certain propositions and in

collective worship supposes that these are widely shared by those in the assembly hall. (1989, p1)

Some religious groups have complained that the nature of worship in schools undermines the true value of worship for believers because it trivialises an important aspect of their religious life.

Others, however, would counter this argument by declaring that there is a vast difference between worship as it occurs in faith communities and that which goes on in school. The term 'collective' is thus used to distinguish the particular kind of worship which is appropriate in schools from that which occurs in faith communities. The word collective in this context dates back to the 1944 Act when worship was seen as something in which all pupils took part at the same time. Worship in schools cannot be described as 'corporate' or 'communal' as these terms contain certain assumptions. 'Corporate worship' is described by the British Council of Churches (1989) as implying one body of worshippers, whereas 'collective worship' implies, 'the retention of individuality in the context of unity' (p25). It thus recognises that within the school gathering there will be people with varied beliefs. It thus respects the individual and allows each person to make their own response to worship. 'Communal worship' also implies that the body of people are coming together to share similar beliefs.

A further emphasis in the 1988 Act, and one which updates the 1944 Act, is that of the need to make worship appropriate to the particular pupils involved. The role of worship fulfils one of the main aims of education as stated at the beginning of the Education Reform Act, that of promoting the spiritual development of children. In this context worship is seen as educational, and in order to be so, must reflect the needs and experiences of the pupils. Hull (1990) sums up the status of the children:

> They always remain learners. They are never to be treated as believers although the fact that they are or are not believers is certainly relevant to the type of educational worship which will be provided. (p66)

We have seen that schools are able to match worship to ages and abilities in the way they organise worship, but they must also match it to their family backgrounds. This means they must take into account children from practising Christian and other religious homes, non-practising homes, and homes in which there is no religious background. The worship in schools must be modelled on the children, not vice versa. This means that worship is going to vary from school to school as each one reflects upon the family backgrounds of its children.

'Wholly or mainly'

This vague term is considered by many to be a new restriction in school worship. Worship is to be 'wholly or mainly of a broadly Christian character'. The DES Circular 3/89 explains this term by adding that 'most acts of worship in a term must be broadly Christian'. In the absence of further definition, it is obvious that this is open to wide interpretation. In some schools it could be interpreted as 51 per cent of acts of worship, in others it could be as much as 99 per cent. Some have interpreted the phrase rather differently. Hull (1990) suggests that it could mean that each assembly need only be mainly Christian, rather than a wholly Christian event (p65). This would open the way for including Christian and non-Christian aspects in any one assembly. This might mean that worship in every assembly could include material from any religious tradition.

If a school interprets the Act by making the majority of its acts of worship broadly Christian, what are the rest to be? The Act does not say, but many feel that this is where other religious traditions can be represented and where aspects of the school's values and concerns can be explored. McCreery (1991) found that among head teachers there was a variety of interpretations given to this clause. Schools felt that their worship could be described as broadly Christian even where they did not contain specifically religious materials. They were also concerned to cater for the non-Christian pupils in the school and so made sure they included material such as stories from other religious traditions.

'Broadly Christian'

This is possibly the most controversial part of the Act's clauses on worship, and one which religious groups in particular have been especially concerned about. There are various reasons for the inclusion of the word 'Christian'. As we have seen there was concern in the House of Lords that Christian children were being deprived of the experience of worship. It is suggested that this was either because many assemblies were now secular with no religious in-put or because of the multi-faith worship adopted in many schools. The 1944 Act had not made any mention of the word 'Christian'. This reflects the broad nature of that Act but also reminds us of the fact that in 1944 a Christian education was still considered the norm. During the debate leading up to the 1988 Act, the members of the House of Lords were emphatic that they did not wish to indoctrinate or nurture all children in Christianity and they were keen to point out that other religions should be able to provide worship for their own children. So what is to be made of the inclusion of this term?

Many would argue that we must interpret this term as widely as possible if we are to find a workable pattern for schools. Firstly, acts of worship need only 'reflect' broad traditions of Christian belief. There is an ambiguity here which allows for a variety of responses. Secondly worship must reflect 'broad traditions' of Christian belief. The British Council of Churches (1989) urges teachers to interpret this widely to include the wide variety of Christian traditions. This could include Quaker, Anglican and Methodist traditions, and is thus a guard against sectarianism. The way is also left open for presenting children with a variety of styles including meditation, silence and song. It is felt that much of the current practice in schools will still be in line with the Act as many assemblies could be said to reflect broad traditions of Christian belief even where there is no explicit mention of Christian material.

Some feel that the intention of the Act is more strict than this and that the legislators envisage something much more akin to the traditional model of worship of the past. Some also bemoan the fact that Christianity is seen as the 'norm' with other religions being seen as lesser alternatives. Hull (1990) identifies a new confessional element in the legislation which has not been seen before (p64).

It has been found (McCreery, 1991) that head teachers have mixed views about interpretation of the Act. One head recognised the opportunity for including faiths other than Christianity by interpreting the term 'broadly Christian' in a wide way. He regretted the fact that the Act did not identify what was meant by 'worship' as it left both him and his staff unsure about what should be done. Another head was so appalled at the document that she immediately applied to the SACRE for an exemption from Christian worship for the whole school.

Withdrawal from worship

Schools must make parents aware of their right to withdraw their children, and parents can, if they wish, provide alternative forms of worship. If they wish they may take the children elsewhere for worship providing that:

- The child could not reasonably attend a school of the appropriate faith or denomination;
- suitable arrangements have been made;
- it does not interfere with the child's access to the rest of the school curriculum except at the beginning or end of a school session. (Warwickshire, 1990, p36)

Parents can also request alternative provision within the school but this must not take the place of the non-denominational worship, nor put the school to extra expense. It should also be in line with the curriculum within the school.

Teachers in county schools also have the right to withdraw from assembly on grounds of conscience and they need to make this intention clear to the head teacher. Head teachers also have the right to withdraw, but because they have overall responsibility for worship they must ensure that the law is followed within their school.

Standing Advisory Councils on Religious Education

The 1988 Act has made it compulsory for local authorities to establish SACREs. Part of their role is to advise the local authority on religious education and worship, but they have a specific duty in relation to collective worship. They must consider requests from head teachers for a determination that the worship in their school should not be broadly Christian in nature. It is they who decide whether either the whole school or groups within it are exempt from Christian worship.

The SACRE must also report annually to the National Curriculum Council, giving an account of the advice they have offered to the local authority over the year. However, the SACREs have no direct power regarding worship even though they will be acting as 'Watchdogs' (Cox and Cairns, 1989) of the local authority.

So far we have examined the Act from the point of view of educationists who have various connections with school life. We have seen that the Act is open to a variety of interpretations and that some are more positive about it than others. What of faith communities? How have people with a personal religious viewpoint responded to the Act?

The responses of religious communities

It has already been suggested that many within religious traditions would rather not see worship in school because they feel it devalues the whole concept of worship. Others have been content with the provision of the 1944 Act because it was sufficiently vague to allow for a variety of practices. Parents who were unhappy with provision had the option of removing their children from worship. Now there are those within religious groups who are openly hostile to the changes. The hostility tends to centre around the inclusion of the word 'Christian'. The arguments from educationists for a wide interpretation of the terms is little consolation when the word 'Christian' comes glaring from the page.

Many religious groups are pleased to see the recognition of a spiritual side of life and the recognition that education needs to include religious teaching to develop the whole child. Some though are disappointed at what they see as an opportunity missed and have grave concerns about the implications of the Act.

In Cox and Cairns (1989), a Christian, Jean Walker, regrets the fact that other faiths have no positive inclusion in the Act. She is also concerned that the Church of England has retained its privileged position on SACREs. She hopes that children will not receive an inaccurate picture of what worship means to a faith community. On the positive side she welcomes the possibility of the Act to develop the spiritual growth of children and believes that Christians will do their best to work within the Act (p87).

In my own study (McCreery, 1991) a head teacher at a school with children from many different backgrounds spoke of the response of some of the Christian parents. He said they were unhappy about what they saw as the undermining of their cultural heritage. Christian parents in other schools have recently been involved in disputes with local authorities about the inclusion of material from other faiths.

Parents from other faiths are equally concerned about what they see as the elevated position of Christianity. They feel that their children are losing out. Where a school has an exemption from Christian worship there is the assumption that it will be replaced by some form of multi-faith worship. Thus it is seen that whereas Christian children can receive Christian worship, non-Christians will only receive multi-faith worship. There is also the feeling that many parents are being discouraged from removing their children from worship and some religious communities provided parents with forms to fill in to present to the head teacher requesting withdrawal.

Another group who have found difficulty with the Act are Humanists. For many years Humanists have been able to take part in discussion on worship through SACREs and have found that the pattern of worship as it appears in schools has been acceptable. Now some are less confident because of the 'Christian' inclusion. Some see it as a backward step, undermining years of discussion and progress.

Developments since 1988

Since the passing of the 1988 Act there has been time to reflect on its requirements and assess the implications for schools. It can be seen that there are a variety of interpretations and that not everyone is satisfied with the terms. It is clear that schools themselves must find a way of working with the Act to provide the most appropriate form of worship for their children. Teachers too must take time to reflect on the requirements to examine their own standpoint. They must then decide whether their consciences prohibit them from taking part.

One indication of the effect of the Act has come from the annual reports of the SACREs as published by the National Curriculum Council. In the 1992 report it was noted that nine schools had requested and been granted determinations exempting them from Christian worship, compared with 38 in the 1991 report. This small number might suggest that now that schools are familiar with the Act they have been able to find a pattern of worship which they feel fulfils the terms. Few SACREs had mentioned pupils being withdrawn from worship, and those that did reported that numbers were small. Work was going on within schools to discuss the flexibility of worship with parents and local communities. Five SACREs had monitored worship within the schools and had found problems with the practicalities of organising worship every day, finding teachers willing to lead worship, and the variable quality of worship. Many SACREs and local authorities were busy producing guidelines and resources for schools regarding worship. These reports indicate the on-going attempt within schools to address the issues of collective worship.

A further development on worship since 1988 is the Government White Paper 'Choice and Diversity for Schools' which was published in July 1992. Chapter 8 of this paper proposes new legislation to give impetus to the development of RE. It begins, 'The Government will continue to emphasise the importance of the school's role in promoting pupils' spiritual and moral development through its teaching and pastoral care' (p37).

The main provisions concern grant-maintained schools and their freedom to adopt any local authority syllabus, and to be represented on SACREs. However, there is also concern to reiterate the terms of the 1988 Act regarding RE and worship. The White Paper says, 'Proper regard should continue to be paid to the nation's Christian heritage and traditions in the context of both religious education and collective worship provided in schools' (p37). At the time of writing, the outcome of these proposals is unknown. However, results of a survey on RE and worship published under the headline, 'Schools flout law on worship' in the *Times Educational Supplement* (December 25th 1992), suggest that there is still confusion and suspicion over the role of worship in schools. It suggests that many schools are not fulfilling the terms of the 1988 Act, with only 40 per cent of the primary schools contacted providing worship at least four times a week. The rest were providing less. Schools still seemed to be wary of what they see to be the Government's intention of making assembly an explicitly Christian activity.

One thing that is clear is that collective worship in schools is here to stay for the immediate future. The next few years may see changes in the practice of school worship as schools adapt it to the changing needs of their schools. The 1988 Act has established a few ground rules for the provision of worship but it leaves a lot of questions unanswered. It explains how often worship is to take place and it gives a vague picture of what it should be like. What it does not do is explain the purpose or the value of worship or suggest what acts of worship should consist of. What is the value of worship? Why is it important in the education of young children? What activities constitute worship? How do we do it? For answers to these questions we must look elsewhere. There are several places we can go to and these will be explored in subsequent chapters.

CHAPTER 3
The Value and Purpose of Collective Worship

Introduction

In the previous chapter the main requirements of the 1988 Act were outlined, together with an explanation of the ways in which they have been interpreted in subsequent literature. It was seen that the Act describes the practical organisation of collective worship and some idea of what it should contain; but it does not attempt to identify what the purpose of worship is, or what value it has for children's education. If we are to make sense of this activity we must seriously consider what it is we are trying to achieve by it. In National Curriculum subjects clear goals are set, outcomes are defined and achievement levels are set out; but the 1988 Act makes no such provision for collective worship, and schools are left to decide on the value it has for their children. There is an implicit assumption that in some way collective worship is an essential part of children's education but no attempt is made to explain why. The Government's White Paper 'Choice and Diversity' (July 1992) made reference to the role of worship in school, saying, 'Religious education and collective worship play a major part in promoting the spiritual and moral dimension in schools' (p37). This directly relates to the intentions of the Government to provide a 'broad and balanced curriculum' which promotes the spiritual, moral, cultural, mental and physical development of pupils. For further information, however, teachers have to consult the various books, publications and guidelines which have been produced since 1988.

In this chapter the value and purpose of collective worship is explored. Why should it be part of children's education? How do they benefit from it? How does it help prepare them for the world of work and the society of which they will become an important part?

These questions will be answered in a number of ways.

1. In order to discuss the value of worship there needs to be an

understanding of what is meant by the term 'worship' in the school context.

2. Next we can explore various suggestions which have been put forward regarding value and purpose.

3. From here we can examine various issues which arise from such suggestions in order that schools can identify their own position and begin to see a positive way forward in the understanding of the subject.

To do this we will be examining the suggestions put forward in recent literature, supplementing this with views from teachers and children.

What do we mean by worship in school?

As discussed in previous chapters the place of worship in schools has been established since the earliest days of state education. When the 1944 Act made collective worship compulsory it was simply reflecting what was common practice in schools.

> In legislating for a daily act of collective worship for all pupils, the 1944 Education Act merely consolidated and enforced existing educational practice, and put the seal of confirmation on the Christian philosophy of education. (Slee, 1990, p6)

Because it served to induct children into the Christian church, much school worship reflected the prevalent pattern of worship in churches. The Durham Report (1970) describes the picture of the time very clearly: 'In many primary and secondary schools, Assembly consists of a hymn; a reading from the bible, or from some inspirational literature; prayers and the Lord's Prayer' (p130). It is this 'church' image of school worship which has remained in the consciences of many teachers today, and not surprisingly those teachers are very wary of participating in such an activity where it conflicts with either their personal beliefs and/or their view of education.

There are those who would argue that this traditional view of worship is narrow and antiquated, and that schools in a multi-faith society need to take a much wider interpretation of the word 'worship'. Two contrasting models of worship have been identified, the second of which is considered to be of relevance in relation to school as an educational institution.

Two models of worship

A person's understanding of the term worship will depend on his or her religious, cultural and scholastic experiences. There can therefore be many interpretations of the word. Worship as understood by Buddhists will be very different to Muslim understanding. Slee (1990) describes two models of worship which have implications for schools. In the first sense it is an explicitly religious concept which demands commitment to a certain set of beliefs. Worship in churches and other places of worship is usually interpreted in this way. In the second sense it takes on a much wider meaning, based on the Anglo-Saxon origin of the term which was *Weorth-scipe* i.e. *Worth-ship*. This model places emphasis on the celebration of shared values, that is 'That which is of worth to the community'. It is argued that in many schools, this second model has emerged over the years, replacing the first model. Head teachers will often describe what they believe is going on in assembly in these terms. In a survey of school worship which I undertook (McCreery, 1991) one head said, 'I wouldn't call it worship, what we do. I would call it 'Worth-ship' (p24).

This move away from the traditional, Christian model is also seen in recent documents produced by SACREs (Standing Advisory Councils on Religious Education) in their guidelines for schools. For instance, Wandsworth SACRE states that worship should, among other things, 'give expression to the common values which underpin the school's existence as a community' (p2).

It has been suggested (Hull, 1975; Slee, 1989; White, 1989; Wandsworth, 1990) that this second model of worship identifies the way forward for collective worship in schools if the activity is to be of educational value. Non-religious schools are not worshipping communities. It is not just that they house people from very different backgrounds, but that it is not part of their agenda to initiate children into a particular faith.

It is necessary to say here that the focus of this book is collective worship in non-religious schools. Voluntary schools, such as Church of England, Roman Catholic and Jewish schools, are permitted by law to provide teaching in their faith. Worship in such schools is likely to be of a different, more confessional nature. This, more restricted sense of the word worship, however, as used in places of worship, cannot be applied to worship in schools with no religious foundation for several reasons:

1. It presupposes the truth of a particular set of religious beliefs.
2. It contradicts the philosophical foundation of western education leaving it open to charges of indoctrination.
3. It fails to take into account the variety of religious and non-religious backgrounds of children, parents and teachers.

4. It makes compulsory an activity which by its nature should be voluntary.
5. It can give children a distorted picture of what it is like to worship in a faith community.

If the traditional model of worship is rejected together with its explicit aim of inducting children into one particular faith, what then is left? What purpose can we find for this activity? The answer, as we have seen, lies in the wider 'worth-ship' interpretation of the word, and it is this model which will now be explored in order to identify value and purpose in this most controversial area of school life.

Worship as a unifier

The capacity of worship to hold communities together is recognised as a major value of collective worship among head teachers and their staff. Worship is seen as a time when different groups of children meet together as a single body. It is a time when classes, so often in a little world of their own, can be seen as part of the larger all-embracing community. Teachers too are able to leave the isolation of the classroom and see themselves, as well as their classes as part of a homogeneous group. That group is the community of the school.

Whatever the backgrounds of pupils or staff, whatever their religious, economic, cultural backgrounds, the one thing they have in common is membership of the school community. In this way collective worship can serve as a means by which individuals can share a common identity. In a whole school assembly, the whole community is gathered and the different groups can be made aware of their role in the whole structure while smaller group assemblies enable children of similar ages to identify their common concerns and interests.

On this argument, the value of the school coming together is clearly lost if assembly is seen as useful non-contact time for some of the most important members of that community. It is a pity that assemblies are sometimes used to give teachers much needed time to attend to other things, for this might suggest to children that assembly is an unimportant time, a device to occupy children while staff get on with more important jobs. The value is also lost if large numbers of children are withdrawn from assembly. This promotes a feeling of elitism, where only certain members of the school belong to the community and others are outsiders. This concern is reflected in the Wandsworth SACRE's document (1990) which states:

> Collective Worship should be inclusive not exclusive. It should be an occasion

when all feel that they can contribute, all can gain and all feel valued as persons, whatever their belief system or life style. (p2)

Why is this unifying aspect of worship valued in schools? In the study which I undertook (McCreery, 1991), several reasons were given by staff and children. Not least was the feeling that assembly is the only time in the school day when all groups can come together to discuss issues outside the academic concerns of the classroom. Schools feel it can help to minimise the differences between children so that they learn to see what things they have in common, rather than what makes them different. In this role it might contribute towards the school's equal opportunities and anti-racist policies. One head teacher spoke of the value of 'togetherness'. Another spoke of an interview with a parent who wanted to withdraw her child: 'I said to her, if you withdraw your children you're withdrawing them from a very important part of the unifying aspects of our school'. Staff also saw worship as a unifier in the sense that it is an activity in which children are not in competition, less able children being able to contribute as much as more able.

As part of children's preparation for the outside world, collective worship is seen as enabling them to understand the concept of community. They may then be able to apply this to the communities they belong to outside school. Key themes in assemblies, such as 'togetherness', 'responsibilities', 'roles', 'strengths and weaknesses', can all contribute to children's awareness of what it means to *belong*. This might be the school they belong to, their local community, religious group, the European community or even the community of the world. They can begin to see the nature of those common bonds which link people together. For instance, in an assembly which I observed in one multi-faith school the children discussed the problems of refugees in the world. When asked afterwards what they had learned they gave answers such as, 'Not to be greedy, to think of others, what's in the news, about other people'.

Worship as a celebration of shared values

Linked very much to the sense of the unifying force, and an aspect which clearly illustrates the 'worth-ship' concept, is the value of worship for celebrating shared values. One of the problems which people have about worship in school is that the children come from so many different backgrounds. The question is asked, 'How can we all worship together, when we all believe in different things?' The answer is found in the emphasis on *collective* rather than corporate worship.

If the school is to come together for worship it must be something which all can accept. Within a faith community this is not a problem, because even if all members of the congregation do not believe everything which is said or done, they broadly agree with what goes on and it is their choice to attend. In school, collective worship is compulsory and so what is said must reflect the beliefs of the people attending. The only way to do this is to make worship a celebration of those values which everyone in the school can be expected to share. Whatever groups children belong to outside, the school is the community, and so worship will be a celebration of 'That which is of worth to this community'.

This is clearly seen in assemblies where concepts such as love, sharing, responsibility and respect are explored. In my study, one teacher described worship as an opportunity for everybody 'to think and question their own attitude to what is of value to others as well as themselves'. Of course, as part of such work it is expected that schools will want to use material from religious traditions, and there is nothing in the 1988 Act to prevent this. Such material will probably be chosen to reflect the particular traditions which are represented in the school. In many cases religious material may form a key part of assemblies, but the difference between using the material in this way compared to the traditional way is the purpose to which it is put. The material will not be used to extol the 'truth' of one particular faith, rather it will be used to explore the response of a religion to the concept which is being studied – for example, how a particular religion interprets 'responsibility' or 'love' in its precepts and practices.

It is not suggested that this aspect of worship will be trouble-free. In discussing values there will almost certainly be some controversial issues raised. An attitude is needed in which members of the community can feel confident in expressing their views about certain topics. This is where the presence of a positive school ethos is vital. In a church school this might be easily identifiable within the context of the religious tradition. For example, Sullivan (1990) points out the importance of the distinctive ethos of Catholic schools. He uses references from church documents to illustrate this feature of school life. 'The Gospel spirit should be evident in a Christian way of thought and life which permeates all facets of the educational climate' (p25) (taken from the document *The Religious Dimension of Education in a Catholic School*, 1988). State schools, however, have no such identifiable foundation and so ethos is more likely to be developed as a result of the efforts of the head teacher, staff and the rest of the community. Where a positive ethos exists, the values of the school community are more easily identified. For example if a school is active in its insistance on respect for the individual, this can be part of the shared values of the school and explored explicitly in collective worship. I found that head teachers when interviewed were quickly able to identify those values which were shared by the school community and which found expression in collective worship. Values such as trust, honesty, hope, respect, tolerance, dignity, caring, appreciating, featured regularly among interviewees in my study. Warwickshire SACRE (1989) recognises the importance of worship in reflecting on ethos:

> A gathering of a school community which can embrace teachers, pupils and occasionally other staff, parents, governors and visitors from the wider community will naturally provide a centre to reflect the ethos of the school. (p5)

Of course, a healthy discussion of controversial issues will not only reflect the school ethos, but also help to mould its characteristics. On the one hand, matters on which there may be disagreement can be more confidently aired in a school that has built up an ethos of trust and respect; on the other hand, assembly serves as an important opportunity to generate and reinforce a school ethos which reflects values such as these. It is a chicken-and-egg situation in which the school is not a static entity, but is constantly being developed by the attitudes perpetrated by the head and staff, especially in assembly.

Worship as time for reflection

Schools are busy places. At any one time there is so much going on that it is difficult to identify the many facets of school life. Staff are often so inundated with various internal and external demands, and children may be so preoccupied in working away on a variety of topics, that there is rarely time to stand back, take a breath and review the situation. Collective worship can fulfil an important function here, providing a moment of calm among the hustle and bustle. At whatever time of day it is held, it can offer a quiet time when there is time to reflect on wider issues – a time not always available in the atmosphere of the classroom. Currently, schools are so concerned with National Curriculum subjects that other areas of human experience can be neglected and there is the danger that children never see the common links in what they do.

I once asked a group of students, at the beginning of their initial teacher training, what they felt schools needed to teach children. Their answers were surprising. They did not list academic subjects or focus on 'basic skills'. Instead they listed those things which many would consider to be part of the 'hidden curriculum'. Among the items were, tolerance, developing relationships, co-operation and so on. Most teachers would agree that these aspects are essential to school life and would hope that they are being developed in an implicit if not explicit way. Collective worship offers a time when these qualities can be addressed explicitly. In this way worship will complement the work of the classroom, particularly in subjects such as personal and social education.

If we examine some typical features of assembly we see that the structure is often already there for this time of reflection. Often assembly takes place in a room different from the regular classroom. A physical break from the academic environment is made. A particular atmosphere is set as children are asked to assemble quietly or even in silence. Music often contributes to the establishment of this atmosphere. This may be the only occasion in the school day when there is an atmosphere of solitude. The value of such a quiet time should not be underestimated. Adults value quiet periods to think, pray, meditate, relax and to reflect. Children too can be encouraged to view this time positively. Waddup (in Bastide, 1992) says,

> There must be space in the school day for the child to feel secure by him/herself, to sit quietly either singly or in a group and to be led to feel safe with silence. (p33)

The topics which are explored in assembly *demand* time for reflection. It is not a time merely to pass on knowledge, it is a time for reflecting on the impact that knowledge has on individuals' lives. The topics may relate to the children's personal lives in or out of school, as well as to events in the community and the world at large. Collective worship is the time for children to think about their own response to such events.

Worship as preparation for corporate worship

Earlier, it was suggested that we cannot, in an educational institution, demand that children worship in the traditional sense of the word. Some would also say that because of what is known about children's conceptual development, it is unlikely that they would actually worship in this sense (Hull, 1975). It is, however, suggested that through collective worship in school children can be introduced to the concept of worship as part of their religious education. In assemblies, therefore, children would be learning what it means to worship. John

Hull coined a phrase which has been widely used to describe this activity. The concept of bringing children to the 'threshold of worship' describes the act of helping children to understand what it means 'to worship'. The aim is not to bring them to worship but to acquaint them with some of the ritual, language and beliefs employed by faith communities in their corporate acts of worship.

This approach is seen in some of the guidelines for worship produced by local authorities. Wandsworth SACRE (1990), for example, states that worship is

> To provide experiences which strengthen attitudes and dispositions in all pupils so that those with a religious commitment may worship more adequately and the uncommitted may develop a capacity at least to approach the threshold of worship. (p2)

Embedded in this view is the idea that to understand the role of worship is an important part of children's religious education. Some would say that this suggests that the ability to worship is part of the goal in children's education, and they would take issue with the idea that it would be 'a good thing' if children did 'learn to worship'. Those who are wary of this position of collective worship may take reassurance from John Hull's summary of the aims of collective worship. It appears fourth in his list.

> To provide some experience and understanding of what worship is so that the way of worship, along with other life styles, will remain an option for anyone who wishes to follow it and so that all will have some insight into what it is like to live a religious life. (Hull, 1975, pp118–19)

Worship as part of spiritual development

> A broad and balanced curriculum is one which promotes the spiritual, moral, cultural, physical and mental development of the pupils.

This is how the official commentary on the 1988 Education Reform Act (DES Circular 3/89) begins its description of the basic curriculum. To date much of what has emerged since 1988 has tended to focus on the mental development of children in terms of subject areas, a concentration which has tended to overshadow some of the other considerations. So far, the spiritual and moral and perhaps even the cultural appears only implicitly in the National Curriculum.

Collective worship can be seen as explicitly addressing the spiritual aspect of children's education. Gent (1989) describes the spiritual as 'concerning the essence, the inner realities of things – realities which, by definition, are often hidden' (p10). He goes on to suggest that searching for the spiritual is an activity which can be taken into the exploration of science or in identifying the 'spirit' of the school. In all schools there needs to be discussion as to whether there is a valid role for schools to play in developing spiritual understanding in children, and, if so, whether this is sufficiently recognised in the curriculum provided for children. The term 'spirit' is widely used in everyday language. We speak of being in 'high spirits' or the 'spirit of adventure' or the 'human spirit'. Obviously it is also used in religious contexts too. The head teachers whom I interviewed also recognised this aspect of existence, although they often had difficulty describing it. One head spoke of, 'something that's out of this world' and 'an out-of-world experience'; another said, 'I do believe we all have spirits and a spiritual awareness definitely needs developing'.

Needless to say, it will be difficult for staff to take on the development of the spiritual if they do not believe it exists. Yet if a school is to engage in helping pupils towards an understanding of the concept of worship, some awareness of what people recognise as 'spiritual' would seem essential. Recent work by David Hay (e.g. *Exploring Inner Space*, 1987) and others seem to suggest that a great number of people have had experiences which they find they cannot explain in rational terms and they, therefore, recognise a spiritual side of life. As part of the purpose of collective worship, children can be made aware that there are some events in people's lives which they attribute to the spiritual realm.

Problems of commitment

By law, both children and teachers can withdraw from collective worship. These conscience clauses, which are in both the 1944 and 1988 Acts, are there to prevent personal beliefs from being compromised. Such compromise can easily be a problem where worship is understood in its narrowest sense, where commitment to a particular set of religious beliefs is assumed. Is it still a problem within the wider interpretation, which was discussed earlier, that of 'worth-ship'? The set of beliefs to which there must be commitment here are those established within the context of the school. This set of beliefs in theory should encompass all members of the school community so that no-one should feel the need to withdraw.

When the 1988 Act was passed, with its renewed emphasis on school worship, there was a great deal of concern that the new terms would lead to hundreds of parents withdrawing their children from this activity. As we saw earlier, however, according to the analysis of SACRE reports by the National Curriculum Council (1991; 1992), this does not appear to have happened. One reason for this could be that schools have been able to reassure parents that collective worship will still focus on those values which are shared by the whole school community.

There are teachers who are very uncomfortable with the notion of worship in the context of their personal beliefs. One teacher in my survey said that, because she had no religious commitments, she saw no value in the exercise. This assumption that personal commitment to a faith is a necessary pre-requisite for taking part in assembly is a common one. In the Culham Report (1992) there are several comments from teachers on this theme: 'We do a good job in developing the spiritual needs of the children. It does help if the head teacher and his staff are practising Christians' (p27). Another, however, did not agree, saying: 'I feel strongly that the values of honesty, truth, justice, and fairness which are common to all religions (and Humanist thinking) should be promoted . . . This is what we try to do. The Christian teachers take this from the religious angle, others take it from non-religious bias' (p16).

Ultimately it will be up to individual teachers to decide whether they are able to take part. The main issue, however, is how far a teacher is committed to the idea of collective worship in the 'worth-ship' sense rather than to any particular religious tradition. As another respondent in the Culham Report said, the effectiveness of collective worship depends on 'ensuring the staff are committed to it. If they are not the lesson learned by the children will be negative' (p27).

A related point to consider is whether it should always be those with a religious commitment who are the ones to lead collective worship. Given the argument that school worship is more about the celebration of shared values than a demonstration of adherence to a particular faith, there should be a place for those without a religious commitment to be able to explore their views with the children. If staff find themselves unable to participate in or lead collective worship in a particular school, perhaps questions need to be asked why. Perhaps what is being offered in the school is of a nature which excludes certain groups. If it is, then the school needs to work towards a more inclusive form of collective worship. If staff feel strongly about this then it is up to them to work for an improvement in provision. This can only be done from the inside. Those who opt out of collective worship altogether will never be in a position to develop and improve it.

Conclusion

In this chapter an attempt has been made to identify the value and purpose of collective worship in schools today. What emerges is a form of worship which is peculiar to schools. It does not have its basis in any religious community, but the educational process of the school. Some would say that what has been described is not worship. They may be right. It is certainly not worship in its strictest sense, but as we have seen that kind of worship is problematic as part of compulsory education. The other alternative would be to provide separate acts of worship for the different religious groups represented within the school. Although this might be possible within the terms of the Act, especially where parents have requested alternative provision, it would be contrary to the spirit of the Act in its call for *collective* worship. But, more importantly, a situation in which each religious group files into its own room, is not one which many schools would wish to see since it institutionalises division and separateness, rather than unity and common life. Collective worship in schools must first and foremost be educational rather than evangelical, contributing to the education of all the children.

CHAPTER 4
The Content and Presentation of Worship

Introduction

The previous chapter was concerned with the purpose of collective worship and how important it is to identify exactly what it is we are trying to do. This chapter is concerned with putting those purposes into action and exploring what should be the content of collective worship.

It has been seen that the traditional model of school worship was structured very much on the kind of worship which takes place in a Christian church. The content often reflected Christian teaching, and the presentation of that teaching was often in the form of a Bible reading, some explanation of that reading, a hymn and a prayer. In recent years there has been a move towards a more creative approach which is more child-centred and which attempts to provide for the majority of the school population. This chapter will explore the possibilities for the content and presentation of school worship in the light of the 1988 Act and the suggestions for purpose outlined in the previous chapter.

The 1988 Act requires collective worship to be, 'wholly or mainly of a broadly Christian character'. There is no explanation of what a 'broadly Christian' assembly should look like or contain. It is up to schools to decide how they interpret this. Furthermore there is no explanation of what those assemblies which are not 'broadly Christian' should contain. Schools can find assistance from the guidelines being published by their local authorities and Standing Advisory Councils on Religious Education (SACREs). Wandsworth SACRE states, 'We are not told that school worship should conform to Christian liturgy, nor that it shall simply be "Christian" ' (1990, p2). Many schools have found that the kinds of assemblies they provided prior to the 1988 Act are still appropriate under the terms of the Act.

Schools may find that there is little difficulty in fulfilling this requirement:

> Since the commonly held social values which schools seek to promote largely derive from the historical and cultural influence of Christianity, there should be no difficulty in meeting this requirement. (CEM Theme 15, 1992)

In that proportion of assemblies which are not 'broadly Christian', schools are at liberty to explore other religious traditions, presumably in the same kind of 'broad' sense in which Christianity is covered. Of course if a head teacher applies to the SACRE for a determination for exemption from Christian worship, then the content of assembly will be decided by the school. They will then be expected to present worship which reflects 'broad traditions' of something other than Christianity.

Over the years many schools have developed creative and interesting ways of presenting worship using a variety of topics thought appropriate for their children. This next section explores the many topics which have been used and begins to identify ways in which topics can be linked to the rest of the curriculum.

Using themes as the content of worship

As with any other school activity the content of worship needs careful consideration. I am not fond of collections of one-off assemblies randomly selected from a book. One would not adopt such an approach when teaching mathematics, and it is essential that worship is planned as carefully as other aspects of the school curriculum. There are many ways to select appropriate assembly material which is relevant to the children in the school. These may arise from a variety of sources such as the time of year, issues in school, national events and so on. This is very much in line with the 1988 Act which demands that worship takes into account the family backgrounds, ages and abilities of the children. In the sections below, it can be seen that themes can be taken from events from within the school, the local community, the world at large and from religious traditions. They are grouped under three headings; events, the world around us, and feelings, attitudes and beliefs.

EVENTS

in the news	diaries
the seasons	exploring the past
religious festivals	exploring the future
secular festivals	harvest
birthdays	journeys
a new year	red letter days
end of term	turning points
beginnings	war and peace
celebration	

THE WORLD AROUND US

achievement	life on Earth
blindness and sight	light and darkness
books	listening
change and decay	messages
the child	mysteries
circles	the natural world
colours	new life
communication	noise
conservation	one planet
creation	parents and children
day and night	patterns
discovery	people with a purpose
education	pollution
eternity	rebirth
fashion	the school
films	science
finding the way	searching
food	sight and seeing
the global village	silence
green	sound
handicap and hardship	stones
health	time
hearing	wealth and riches
heroes	windows
home and family	winners
key people	wonder and awe
language	words
leaders	work and play

FEELINGS, ATTITUDES AND BELIEFS

age	head, heart and hands
aggression	helping hands
anger	hope and despair
barriers	I believe
beauty and the beholder	jealousy
big and small	joy and sorrow
bridges	life and death
caring	love and hate
challenge	my kind of music
choice	obstacles
courage	opportunity
decisions	in others' shoes
dreams	peace and tranquility
experience	power
fantasy and imagination	pride and prejudice
fear	rights
first and last	special things
food for thought	spirit of adventure
forgiveness	strength and weakness
freedom and responsibility	success and failure
freedom and slavery	taking risks
friendship	us and them
fun and enjoyment	value
giving up	victory and defeat
God and gods	ways of seeing
good and evil	what's it worth?
guilt and suffering	why are we here?
happiness	

It can be seen that not only are these lists lengthy but also the topics themselves are very broad in nature. This means that many of them would merit more than one assembly. A whole week or even a term could be spent on some of the items and this idea will be explored further in a later chapter.

Topics such as those suggested not only link with life inside and outside school but also in many cases link with certain areas of the classroom curriculum. The increasing demands of the National Curriculum mean that many teachers will want to explore themes in assembly which directly relate to the work they are doing in class. This is also desirable from the point of view of the purposes of worship.

Links should be drawn between classroom work and assembly to show children the inter-relatedness of school life and to show them that the work they do in the classroom has implications for the way they view life. It is important for children to see that their school work is not value free and that assembly is a good time to reflect on some of the things they are learning about in class.

To help teachers identify the links between curriculum areas, the next section of this chapter takes each of the National Curriculum subjects in turn and identifies some of those themes which could form a link between the work of the classrom and the assembly.

Using the curriculum for content

Themes linked to English

This is probably the easiest area to link with collective worship. The various attainment targets required in English to do with speaking and listening, reading, writing, spelling and handwriting offer a wide variety of opportunities for the assembly.

in the news	books I have read
communication	diaries
education	fantasy and imagination
films	fun and enjoyment
a good read	hobbies
humour	language
messages	my favourite poem
people	red letter days
special books	words
feelings	

Themes linked to science

There are many themes which span the gap between science and religion. A crucial part of science education is enabling children to make decisions and judgements based on evidence. It also has the capacity to develop within children a sense of the wonder of the world. Through science they can begin to recognise that truth claims are based on value judgements and it is in this area of values that science and religion have their links.

achievement	the seasons
beginnings	blindness and sight
change and decay	colours
creation	day and night
discovery	eternity
exploring the future	health
light and darkness	living
mysteries	the natural world
new life	rebirth
stars	searching
sight and seeing	

Themes linked to mathematics

The links between religion and mathematics may not be readily recognisable, but there are some link themes. Maths can be an inspiration for worship in that it can provoke awe and wonder at the complexities of pattern, scale and infinity. Issues of value can be identified in the examination of money and measurement. Number and symbol also play a significant part in religious tradition and language (see Palmer and Breuilly, 1992).

big and small	circles
first and last	patterns
reflection	possible and impossible
signs and symbols	time
turning points	wealth and riches
worth	fair and unfair

Themes linked to history

History plays an important part in the traditions of both religious and secular culture. The National Curriculum demands that children become aware of the values and beliefs behind events of the past.

age	aggression
customs	consequences
change	commitment
fact and fiction	quest
exploring the past	heroes and heroines
key people	leaders and leadership
memories	old and new
past and future	power
strength and weak-	war and peace
ness	victory and defeat
sacred writings	

Themes linked to geography

The idea of holy places features in many religious traditions and children can begin to examine what places are special to them through links with geography and worship. Other geographical areas such as physical geography can also be explored through collective worship. The language of geography also has links with worship where it may be used metaphorically, e.g. journey.

the weather	holy places
journey	signs
barriers	rocks and stones
discovery	freedom and slavery
the global village	conservation
the environment	green
leisure	life on Earth
new worlds	one world
the spirit of	wealth and riches
adventure	directions
our town	homes
water	
pollution	

Themes linked to technology

There are many themes which directly link worship and technology. Later in this chapter it will be shown that methods of presentation offer other opportunities for links.

imagination	bridges
change	windows
in your shoes	conflict
food	opportunity
need	explanations
resources	choice
difficulties	advice
good and evil	obstacles
challenge	

Themes linked to music

Music has not only been a feature of religious tradition down the centuries, but it has also been a medium of religious expression. We will see later in the chapter how music can be used to present worship, but here we will focus on those themes which link it to worship.

listening	time
my favourite music	sounds
voices	people
feelings	beauty
silence	

Themes linked to art

Like music, art has direct links with religious expression. The themes listed serve to identify aspects of art which can be explored through worship.

achievement	beauty
colours	feelings
wonder and awe	people

Themes linked to religious education

Last but not least worship is part of children's religious education. Unlike the National Curriculum subjects there are no national guidelines for RE and so themes will be linked to local authorities' agreed syllabuses. Worship enables children to examine those aspects of religion as they affect the individual. It is a time when children can reflect on the significance of the knowledge they acquire in the classroom.

caring	celebration
children	choice
commandments	special times
decision	festivals
forgiveness	giving up
happiness	helping
hope and despair	I believe
key people	life and death
love and hate	outsiders
pride and humility	silence
success and failure	why are we here?

It is not suggested that the themes listed above belong only to that subject area. Nor is it suggested that these are the only links possible. Teachers will be able to identify their own links as they work through the curriculum. Rather, the lists above serve to show that choosing themes for assemblies need not be an arduous task. Teachers do not have to sit for hours on end, dreaming up appropriate material. Instead they can examine their class topics, the calendar, the newspapers and the life around school to choose topics which are of interest and of value to their children.

Which religions?

Many schools, particularly with children from different religious backgrounds, or no religious background, are concerned about including a variety of standpoints within collective worship. In so far as the 1988 Act requires only the majority of acts of worship in a term to be broadly Christian, it is recognised that material from other religious traditions is allowed. The use of themes enables teachers to be flexible in this matter. It also allows discussion about other religious traditions, and schools may wish to reflect the traditions which are represented in their school or local community. Where schools are placed in predominantly Christian areas they may wish to incorporate material from other religious traditions as part of sound educational policy, although there is no obligation for them to do so.

The presentation of worship

Once an appropriate theme is chosen for the assembly, the next important stage is deciding on presentation. The traditional forms of school worship, i.e. Bible reading, explanation, hymn and prayer, have given way in recent years to more flexible, creative forms. However, in many schools the older practices continue, giving rise to frequent criticism from children and teachers alike that assembly is 'boring'. In this section we are concerned with exploring the many different ways in which assembly can be presented, to allow a more effective use of assembly time. Such creativity may involve more thought and preparation but the end results are worth it.

In presenting assembly, the basic principles which govern effective classroom teaching should be observed:

1. Each assembly should have one clearly focused aim.
There is often the temptation to include far too much material in one assembly. It is better if each assembly has just one main teaching point to focus its purpose. This could easily be summarised in one sentence, for example, 'The children will reflect on the value of friendship.' The content of the assembly is therefore chosen specially to achieve this aim.

2. The aim of the assembly must be achievable.
There is little value in identifying an aim which is so wide or complex that it is impossible to gauge if it has been achieved, for example 'Children's spirituality will be developed.' This is more likely to be a long-term aim encased in the general purpose of worship within the school. A more realistic aim might be, 'Children will reflect on what makes them happy' or, 'Children will explore the significance of water in our lives.'

3. Collective worship should be a learning experience.
This should be identified in the aim of the assembly. The learning which takes place should not be limited to knowledge to be gained but include skills, concepts and attitudes to be developed, for example, 'Children will have opportunity to develop skills of silent reflection.' The same educational criteria should be used as in any other area of school life.

4. Assemblies should not be too long.
There is the temptation to make the most of time gathered together, especially when it may have taken a good length of time to assemble the children. There is no guidance in the 1988 Act as to how long an assembly should be, but many schools find that ten to fifteen minutes is all that is needed to convey a particular message.

5. Assemblies should involve a variety of forms of worship.
Use should be made of different aspects of worship which can lead children to the 'Threshold of worship'. These might include song, reading, speech and silence, meditation and so on.

6. Assemblies should evoke feelings and senses associated with worship.

The whole purpose of the assembly is to move, inspire or enlighten children. This will not be achieved if the presentation is so drab that children are left disinterested. Added to this there must be within the assembly a clear sense that worship is taking place. There are no official criteria for deciding what constitutes 'worship' and it can be interpreted flexibly, as we have seen, but in order to stay within the Act 'worship' should be the primary purpose.

7. *Children should be active not passive.*

In no other curriculum area is it considered good practice for children to be asked merely to sit and be talked at, and yet this is often a feature of assembly. The presentation of the assembly should demand that children are active in that they are invited to respond to the theme. This does not have to mean that the children have to be physically active either in talk or movement (although sometimes they will be) but they should be mentally active.

8. *Collective worship should not demand that children join in with activities which they don't understand or that compromise their own beliefs.*

This has been a failing of assembly in the past. If worship is to follow the terms of the 1988 Act then the children's backgrounds, ages and abilities must be respected.

9. *Each assembly should have a clear structure.*

Just as in lessons teachers ensure that they have a plan, either written or in mind, so should they have a plan for the assembly. Each assembly should have:

- a starting point to get the children's attention;
- an exploration of the theme;
- a conclusion, possibly including time for reflection or celebration.

10. *Collective worship should make use of resources within the school and outside it.*

Teachers need to think widely about the availability of resources for worship. Within school there is a range of audio-visual equipment, objects, books etc which will be of great use. Materials do not need to have been specifically designed for worship.

11. *Acknowledging difference.*

Care must be taken not to present religions as 'all the same':

> To attempt to present a multi-faith act of worship which could be 'all things to all people' would result in something which did justice to no-one. It is necessary to give space to the variety of faiths and philosophies so that they can be fairly represented in an unconfused way. (Warwickshire County Council, 1990)

Ideas for presenting collective worship

In the next section some ideas for presenting worship are outlined. Once again the format is linked with subject areas to show how presenting worship can fulfil some of the requirements of the National Curriculum.

Using English

Story

One of the most useful aspects of English to be used in assembly is that of story. All children from the very youngest to the eldest can respond to story, the power of which is as old as the human race and is one of the best devices for exploring a theme. The choice of stories for collective worship is an important aspect of planning an assembly.

Religious story

Traditionally Bible stories have been the chief material for assemblies. The 1988 Act does not specify that Bible stories must be used but many schools will find them essential for exploring themes. If Bible stories are used then the usual educational criteria must be employed. The teacher must be very clear of the purpose behind their use and be aware of unintentional outcomes. For example, using the parable of 'The Good Samaritan' to explore love for one's enemies must not be allowed to give the impression that only Christians are charitable. Equally important is recognising the ages and abilities of the children. Bible stories often involve concepts which are beyond the understanding of young children. This can lead to the development of negative views of Bible stories or misunderstandings of religious concepts. Teachers would be advised to consider the content of Bible stories as they would any other story to decide if it is suitable for their children. A good example of this concern can be seen in the story of Noah's Ark. This story is widely used in primary schools, particularly where work on water or animals is being done. Focus is usually made on the animals being led into the Ark two by two. What is not often considered is the feature of the story where God is instrumental in the drowning of the rest of the human race. Teachers need to consider the effect this image of God might have on young children.

The 1988 Act also allows for the use of non-Christian material in assembly. Many of the holy writings of other religions include

story material, and where they do the same educational considerations should be used.

In summary the following questions should be asked before
religious stories are used.

1. Does the story contribute to the aim of the assembly?
2. Does the story promote positive feelings about a religious
   tradition?
3. Does the story avoid misunderstandings about religion?
4. Do I understand the meaning and context of the story?

Children's stories

Teachers may find that once they have considered the questions
above and identified their main aim, that contemporary children's
fiction offers a better way of conveying a particular point. Children's
stories need not be a replacement for religious stories, but certainly
offer a valuable alternative. Many children's stories contain features
easily exploited in collective worship. They contain issues of love and
hate, quest, loss, darkness and light, journey and relationships which
are all part of worship. For example, the story of 'The Owl who was
afraid of the Dark' by Jill Tomlinson is an excellent way of
introducing themes of fear or darkness and light.

Religious and non-religious stories alike benefit from one major
feature: the telling rather than the reading of the story. Putting the
story into appropriate language, being able to maintain eye contact
and evoking the right atmosphere are all essential ingredients for the
powerful communication of a story. In large group assemblies it has
the added bonus that the teacher can see the whole group at all times
to see that they are actively involved in the telling. The effective
telling of a story is a desirable skill and teachers should refer to books
and articles which give guidance in this area e.g. *Telling Stories To
Children* by Marshall Shelley (1990, Lion), and 'The Place of Story
in R.E.' by Carole King, which can be found in Bastide (1992). Other
English areas are:

Speaking and listening

Poems, TV, books, reports of visits, role play, telephone conver-
sation, group presentation, newspapers, debate, proverbs, jokes,
interviews, discussion, choral speaking, visualisation, drama, mime,
talent shows, simulation, quiz.

Reading

Holy books, religious writing, poems, quotations, thought for the day, prayers, guided fantasy.

Writing

Presentation of work, creative writing, factual accounts, languages, calligraphy.

Using mathematics

Charts, graphs, presentation, questioning, evaluating.

Using science and technology

Demonstration, presentation, experiments, describing, categorising, display, models.

Using music

Hymns, pop songs, folk songs, chants, singing games, own songs, classical music, with pictures.

Using art and visual stimuli

Pictures, posters, artefacts, natural objects, religious objects, historical objects, works of art, slides, video, film, overhead projector, children's work.

Using movement

Dance, mime, charades, demonstration, animal movement.

Other aspects of presentation

The school and its immediate environment contains a wealth of resources for presenting worship in a varied and stimulating way. Remember that radio, video and TV are often significant features of children's lives and assemblies which relate to popular culture are invaluable. I know a head teacher who uses episodes of the Australian soap opera *Neighbours* to explore issues of relationships in assembly. Her argument is that she knows how many of the children watch the programme every night and are familiar with the story lines. She then uses those story lines to discuss with the children issues of responsibility, caring, love and hate, disappointment, loss and so on.

Hymns and prayers

These aspects of worship have been listed separately because they form an important part of worship within faith communities and are most instantly recognisable as worship. They have been part of traditional school worship for generations and yet they pose the greatest problem for teachers and children in school. The problem is that even if an assembly is broadly Christian and takes into account other faiths without demanding belief, prayer and hymns suggest commitment. There can be a contradiction in an assembly which is based on the shared values of the school and then asks children to take part in these two activities. All the principles upon which the assembly has been based could be negated. To require children to sing, 'Oh, Jesus I have Promised' makes assumptions about the beliefs of those children. Similarly, to demand that children join in with the Lord's Prayer suggests a lack of equality between the faiths. One of the head teachers in my study of three schools reported how a parent complained that her child did not know the Lord's Prayer. The head teacher explained that the philosophy behind assemblies was not to promote one religious tradition in her racially mixed school. It is the responsibility of parents to nurture their children within a particular faith – not the school's. Nor should schools be undermining any religious belief by asking children to join in with specifically religious activities which are contrary to their own beliefs and traditions.

Even so, there is a place for both hymns and prayers in assemblies. One idea, about which I have reservations, is that children can be *invited* to join in with such activities rather than commanded. This could be an acceptable step forward, but it is questionable whether very young children would understand this distinction, particularly when they are used to doing what they are asked to in other areas of school life. A preferable practice, in my view, is to introduce children to prayer and hymns in the main body of the assembly with specific remarks such as, 'This is a song that Christian children sing', or 'Listen to this prayer which Jewish children say'. In this sense the words are 'owned' by a particular group without any suggestion that they are shared by all (Warwickshire County Council, 1990). Children are thus introduced to prayers and hymns without their families' beliefs being compromised. A further use for hymns and prayer in assembly is to acquaint children with the experience of participating in collective singing and prayer. This is needed as part of bringing children to the 'threshold' of worship. However, the songs which they sing need to be carefully chosen from a range of sources and be introduced as 'prayer-like' activities. Instead of the traditional 'Let us pray', children would be invited to listen to the prayer as it reflects the theme of the assembly. Phrases such as 'Listen to the words of this prayer' or 'In a moment of quietness let us think about . . .' or 'Close your eyes and think about what we have learned in assembly' are becoming a frequent feature of school worship. The use of silence is valuable here, allowing children to reflect for themselves on the content of the assembly. In this way prayers can be taken from different religious traditions without compromising belief or undermining the terms of the 1988 Act.

Conclusion

This chapter has been concerned with putting the value and purposes of collective worship within a practical framework. It can be seen that there is a wealth of ideas to be had from a variety of sources. Teachers need not be concerned that worship needs separate planning from the rest of school work as many topics will arise easily from the subjects in the classroom curriculum. In this way worship can be seen to enrich and develop the curriculum by drawing attention to the values and issues which they provoke. A crucial feature of effective worship which is educational and inspirational is the attention needed in presenting it. Through imaginative use of resources and approaches, collective worship can be an exciting, unpredictable, uplifting time in the school day.

CHAPTER 5
Planning for School Worship

Introduction

In the previous chapter, we considered what is appropriate material for school worship. Guidance was given regarding the selection and presentation of suitable topics. In this chapter an outline will be given for planning assemblies for collective worship, going through the stages required for planning an effective assembly.

In the past, school worship has been dominated by a very traditional model which is still evident in some schools today. Yet these assemblies often bear little resemblance to what goes on in the rest of school life. The detailed consideration given to preparing a lesson is often denied to the assembly, which is often a last minute activity where some unsuspecting member of staff is required to address the school for the next ten minutes. It is not all that unusual to see a head teacher or staff member wandering round looking for a Bible five minutes before an assembly begins! Such last minute planning would not be tolerated in curriculum areas and it should not be tolerated for assembly. It goes against all educational principles of preparation, since it ignores any consideration of aims and the idea of progression. Such assemblies are often bleak and directionless, reinforcing in teachers' and children's minds that assembly is an unimportant and meaningless chore. By law collective worship should be provided every day: it is distressing to think that so much compulsory school time may be so wastefully spent.

Under the 1988 Education Reform Act worship should be provided for all pupils (except those who are withdrawn) every day and on the school premises. It can be at any time of the school day in whatever groups the school wishes, e.g. year groups, class groups – but not religious groups. These factors will be the starting point for organising acts of worship.

The next section will outline the possible procedures for planning worship within a school. Naturally they are only suggestions and many schools have their own established traditions for ensuring effective assemblies. There are two main aspects:

1. organising worship across the whole school;
2. planning an individual assembly.

Organising collective worship: some considerations

Assemblies should be seen as special occasions valued by teachers and children alike. They should have a sense of occasion and be times of joy, celebration and serious reflection. In planning assemblies, these ideals should be uppermost in teachers' minds. The preparation behind an assembly will obviously contribute to this sense of occasion. Below is a list of considerations which schools might explore in order to ensure that assemblies are a worthwhile activity.

Setting the right atmosphere

This is an important part of the assembly which needs to be considered beforehand. The room where worship takes place, its furniture, the timing, seating arrangements, all have an impact on the atmosphere generated.

Where is it held?

The 1944 Education Act demanded that the whole school should assemble for worship every day. This meant that most assemblies had to take place in the largest room – usually the hall, gym or dining room. In many primary schools one room has to serve all of these purposes and there is evidence of each activity around the room. Fortunately, the relaxation of this rule in the 1988 Act enables schools to plan assemblies for smaller groups, and so smaller rooms such as classrooms, TV rooms and libraries may be used.

There are several factors which can be considered when deciding upon a suitable venue. The most important of these is the size of the group. For large group assemblies, such as the whole school, the hall is going to be the obvious place. Moving from the classroom to the hall is useful for marking the break between the activity of the classroom and that of assembly, and may help to establish a special sense of purpose. On the other hand, the hall would not be as useful for smaller groups of children who might seem lost in the space, and the possibilities for an intimate atmosphere might be lost. The use of the hall carries further considerations. The time may need to be clearly marked on a school calendar, and caretakers and other members of staff may need to be informed. If the hall is used for a variety of activities the teacher will need to make sure that extraneous equipment is carefully stowed away so that it does not detract from the sense of occasion which you want to promote.

For group assemblies there is more possibility of setting the right atmosphere if a smaller room is used. Many schools have class assemblies which take place in the children's own classroom. Here again efforts must be made to mark some change which indicates the time for worship. Perhaps a particular corner of the room is used, or the children are grouped in a way not usually used in the classroom. An atmosphere for worship will not be established if children are fiddling in their desks, sorting through the book shelves or seeing to the contents of their lunch box!

Whichever room is decided upon, there are other important factors which must also be considered. These include seating arrangements and the setting (see below). Furthermore, interruptions to the assembly should be avoided. This may mean putting notices on doors – particularly in schools where the hall is a through route. Other noises which might disturb may be school bells, the people in the kitchens, outside traffic or telephones.

Seating arrangements

One of the most important considerations in setting the right atmosphere is the seating arrangements. Children who are cramped and crushed or who cannot see or hear what is going on are not likely to sit still, never mind enter an atmosphere conducive to worship. Traditionally children sit in rows in assembly with their class group, usually all facing the front of the hall as the focal point. Some schools, however, provide for more flexible seating arrangements such as horse-shoe shapes or circles. This enables children not only to see the speaker more clearly but each other too.

It is vital that all children can see and hear without difficulty. Special consideration may be needed for children with sight or hearing problems. Remember also that children will only be able to sit on the floor for a short length of time. I recall the cry of an eleven-year-old girl who complained of pins and needles after sitting in assembly so long.

The setting for worship

The setting for worship is also important. The room to be used is likely to be employed for other purposes, and equipment, pictures, views outside the windows may offer distractions to the children. In many assemblies the room is prepared for worship by the addition or special arrangement of certain objects. The focal point is clearly identified by a chair, the TV, screen or table. Fresh flowers, interesting artefacts – either religious or non-religious, displays of pictures, can all serve to focus attention and set a suitable atmosphere.

How the children are treated on their way to, during and after the assembly also gives signals about the nature of the activity. In many schools there is insistence on silence as they enter. Although this is usually part of discipline procedures, it can also serve to encourage the children in silent contemplation. It can be done in a positive manner, for example by asking the pupils to listen to some music as they enter. During assembly some schools allow the children to sit in family or friendship groupings, regardless of their age or class. Again this serves to suggest to children that assembly is a different time from other school activities. When the whole school is gathered together it will be necessary to decide how positive behaviour is encouraged. Memories of teachers patrolling aisles do nothing to enhance the image of assembly. I recall a colleague telling the story of a head teacher who, irritated by the behaviour of one misbehaving child, had bellowed: 'You boy. Stand up. Yes you in the blue jumper', whereupon half of the school stood up: the school uniform was blue!

The timing of assembly

The 1944 Act demanded that each school day should *begin* with collective worship. Once again this is an aspect which has been relaxed by the 1988 Act. Schools can now choose which time of day is most conducive to effective worship. Even so, many schools still decide to hold their assembly in the morning because it is considered valuable to start the day on a positive note, perhaps giving the children a 'Thought for the day' to focus on. A head teacher whom I interviewed said she found that children would often approach her later in the day to offer their own contribution to the theme which had been presented that morning. All the same, using the beginning of the day does have its problems. So often the start of the day is fraught with other concerns, of administration, dinner money, late arrivals, absent staff and other difficulties. This can lead to a hurried arrival at assembly, or a long wait for classes who are not quite ready.

Some schools, therefore, find that other times in the day are more useful. Using assembly to conclude a school session, for example before break or lunch time, can be effective. Some schools find that worship helps to calm the children for the next activity, and so hold assembly perhaps after break. The end of the school day can also be a very valuable time for assembly. Then the children are able to reflect on their activities, sharing work or experiences, and there is a sense of 'rounding off' the day in a positive way. Lastly, there may be certain occasions when the school gathers spontaneously in response to some significant event which arises.

Grouping for assembly

The 1988 Act allows for children to assemble for worship in groups as well as the whole school. This has made things much easier for schools faced with gathering several hundred children together. There is still a place for whole-school worship and many schools have drawn up a pattern for the week involving a mixture of whole school and small group assemblies. The example given below illustrates how the timing and location can vary as well as the criteria for grouping:

MONDAY	WHOLE SCHOOL	9.30	HALL
TUESDAY	LOWER SCHOOL	10.30	HALL
	UPPER SCHOOL	11.00	HALL
WEDNESDAY	YEARS 1 and 2	1.30	LIBRARY
	YEARS 3 and 4	2.00	LIBRARY
	YEARS 5 and 6	2.30	LIBRARY
THURSDAY	CLASSES	12.00	CLASSROOMS
FRIDAY	WHOLE SCHOOL	3.00	HALL

It is important to note that children may not be grouped according to religious affiliation. This would go against the 1988 Act and would be considered educationally undesirable. However, some schools may apply to the local SACRE (Standing Advisory Council on Religious Education) to exempt groups of children from Christian collective worship. In such cases it is permissable to provide alternative forms of worship for these children. Discussion will also need to take place regarding those children whose parents have withdrawn them from worship and how they are to be constructively provided for during assembly time.

The value of being able to group children in a variety of ways is not only of use organisationally, but educationally too. It enables schools to provide worship which is much more in line with the children's intellectual and religious development. The aims, content and presentation of each assembly can be geared to the age ranges present.

Who attends assembly?

In many schools it has been the custom for one person to lead the assembly with only the children present. Students coming back from school experience blocks have sometimes reported that they never saw an assembly because they were told that only the head teacher leading the assembly ever attends. This could be because the time is used as non-contact time for the teaching staff, or because the leader of the assembly would rather not have a wider audience, or because staff, in general, do not wish to be involved in assemblies. Each of these reasons needs examination. Earlier we saw that assembly should be seen as a welcome and valuable time. This is unlikely to be transmitted to the children if some of the most significant people in the school community, i.e. the teachers, are missing. If worship is to celebrate the values of the school community then all members of that community should be present. (Non-teaching staff might also be invited to attend.) It undervalues the experience if the teachers are seen to be involved in 'more important tasks' such as marking or mounting work. Time is precious in primary schools and head teachers are often searching for ways to free their staff, but assembly time is not the place to take this time from. Similarly, it is not appropriate for children to be kept from assembly for extra tuition, or to help teachers in some chore. Once again this undermines the value of assembly, suggesting that it is 'spare' time to catch up on other things.

The second reason for non-attendance of staff, that of reducing the audience, is just as important. While it can be daunting for a teacher, even the head, to face the whole staff as well as the children, it is desirable for him or her to do so. There are two reasons for this. Firstly, all staff need to know what has been covered in assembly so that they can follow up work in the classroom and avoid repetition of material. Secondly, it is essential that everyone knows what goes on in assemblies as part of a monitoring system. If staff do not attend worship, how will they know what is being presented to the children? This could have serious consequences if a particularly enthusiastic teacher gets carried away with her own beliefs. It also enables teachers to get some ideas for presenting their own assembly.

The last reason for non-attendance is perhaps the most significant. If teachers feel they need to withdraw from collective worship in school, there needs to be some discussion as to why. Assemblies should be inclusive, they should not exclude members of the community. The purpose of assembly in school needs to be clearly identified so that all teachers, including those with no particular religious affiliation and those with strong religious commitments, can feel they have a valuable role to play. In this way, assembly is collective for all members of the school, adults included, not just the children.

While it is important for everyone to be involved in worship, the school should also be seen in terms of the wider community. To this end many schools invite parents, governors, religious leaders, local people in general, and ancillary staff to join them in assembly, at least on some occasions. This is a positive approach, strengthening the idea of community and the position of worship as a cohesive force.

Who leads assembly?

In many schools it is still the pattern that the head teacher is the one to lead assemblies. There are a number of reasons for this. Firstly, it is the head who is responsible for seeing that worship takes place in the school. Secondly, many heads see this as an ideal time for contact with the children. Thirdly, it is an opportunity for head teachers to impart some of the values of the school which are often based on his or her philosophy. Fourthly, head teachers are aware of the many demands placed on teachers and so take this job on themselves. Lastly, there is often a shortage of volunteers.

There is certainly value in the head taking on the role of leader in assembly. Free from the day-to-day commitments of the classroom, she is often in a position to have a wider view of issues within the school. The practice also helps children to see worship as a significant activity because the head is involved. In many primary schools the children are taught mainly by one person and this change of 'teacher' can be a refreshing experience. On the negative side, however, children may only associate what goes on in assembly with the head teacher, believing that it has nothing to do with other teachers. They may even get the impression that the head is the only 'religious' person in school, that this assembly business is a peculiar trait of head teachers. In any case, there are other people who can and should be involved in leading assembly, and we shall now look at each of these in turn.

Senior management

Head teachers often employ their deputies and post-holders as assembly leaders as part of their professional responsibilities. This is more beneficial than using just the head alone, and children can see different teachers with their own interests and viewpoints. However, it may still serve to suggest that only those people 'in charge' are interested in worship.

Teachers

There is great value in class teachers leading assemblies, even if only for their own class. They are closest to the day-to-day learning, abilities and interests of the children, and are better placed than the head and senior management team to use assembly as an extension of the regular curriculum. They also have access to a variety of material appropriate for the age range. Moreover, children are able to get to know teachers other than their present class teacher, and respond well to new faces.

Children

The value of using children to lead assemblies should not be underestimated. Children love preparing and showing their work and delight in watching their friends and brothers and sisters at the front. In my study of three schools, children regularly referred to pupil-led assemblies as their favourite. In this context children can share their talents and skills, whether academic, artistic, musical or physical. There are, however, some pitfalls to be avoided. Too often it is obvious that the material presented is not in fact the children's own work. This might be unavoidable with very young children, but older children should certainly be selecting their own content and mode of presentation. Another thing to avoid is the 'Ben Hur' syndrome. This is where class assemblies become so competitive that they become a full-scale epic, each one designed to out-shine the last. The result is children spending a full week or more in heated preparation and rehearsal.

Parents

This is an under-used resource, but one which children will appreciate. Parents offer a different perspective to the professionals within school, yet they are just as close to the interests and abilities of the children. Although perhaps at first hesitant and nervous, parents can produce some exciting and stimulating assemblies. There are many areas of strength which they can draw from including home and work life, family life, cultural background, unusual experiences, special talents, personal interests and so on.

Visitors

There are many people within and outside school who are ideal for presenting assemblies. The list is endless, and includes ancillary staff, school crossing patrol, local charities, school governors, religious leaders, leaders of community enterprises and so on. Each one will have a different perspective and impact on the children. Again some words of caution are needed. Some visitors may not be used to speaking to large groups or groups of children. Every effort must be made to assist visitors and give them access to resources and information. Visitors must also be made aware of the nature of worship within the school. They should not make assumptions about children's religious knowledge or beliefs and they must not use the assembly to promote their own beliefs above others. I have vivid memories of one visitor who frightened the five-year-olds by bellowing, 'And when Jesus comes again, WILL YOU BE READY?' It is essential that other staff are present to keep an eye on the content of the assembly and to assist with discipline and organisation. Every effort must be made to make the visitor welcome and many will come back time and time again to the delight of the children.

Variety

The ideal situation is one where a variety of people lead assembly. Children become used to the idea that different people are involved. They will begin to associate different types of worship with different people, like the community leader who always brings his guitar for songs, or the minister who comes dressed in his special robes. Whoever leads the worship there are some ground rules to be followed. All potential leaders should be warned well in advance of the date and time of their assembly. They should be advised of any current theme and where their assembly fits into this. Resources such as overhead projectors and song books should be readily available for all those involved. Visitors should always be thanked afterwards, if possible by the children themselves.

Long-term planning

So far we have considered the time, place, setting and leading of assembly. Another aspect of organisation which is just as important is the planning of assemblies. This is something which should involve all members of staff, and be related to weekly, termly and even yearly plans. Long-term planning is essential for worship as it helps to build structure and progression into assemblies. It is also vital for achieving a balance between 'broadly Christian worship' and other worship as required by the 1988 Act. It enables staff involved in preparing assemblies to plan around a particular topic and see how their assembly fits into the greater scene. It also avoids repetition and the overuse of material or methods of presentation. Ultimately, planning gives a much more cohesive feel to worship. Instead of one-off, unrelated topics there is a clear purpose in what is being done. Of course this does not deny the opportunity for the one-off assembly in response to a recent event: the planning should be flexible enough to accommodate items in the news, school events, last minute issues.

When planning assemblies across a term the school may wish to consider:

- the time of year, its seasons, school events, national and local events and festivals;
- links with National Curriculum topics and other aspects of the curriculum;
- the religious education syllabus, with appropriate topics for the age range;
- what was covered in the previous term;
- issues of importance in school which can appropriately be addressed in assembly, e.g. playground behaviour and relationships.

Some schools find that themes can be developed across a week, so that each day a new aspect of the theme is explored. The first assembly will introduce the theme and the subsequent days will take a different aspect of it. On the last day the theme is brought to a conclusion. An example of a theme on light which would form part of a planned scheme for assemblies over a term, is given below.

THEME FOR		
THE TERM:	AUTUMN	
THEME FOR		
THE WEEK:	LIGHT	AGE GROUP 6–7 years
MONDAY:	Different types of light.	
	Main aim: to reflect on the variety of sources of light, man made and natural.	
TUESDAY:	Why do we need light?	
	Main aim: to reflect on the many uses to which light is put.	
WEDNESDAY:	Feelings and light.	
	Main aim: to recognise the associations between light and feelings.	
THURSDAY:	Candles on the cake.	
	Main aim: to recognise the symbolism behind the use of candles.	
FRIDAY:	A festival of light e.g. Christmas, Hannukah, Divali.	
	Main aim: to reflect on the use of light in winter festivals.	

Special needs and equal opportunities

Within all planning, consideration needs to be made of those children who may need special provision. In worship this may be a wide variety of children. Organisation should take into account any physical requirements, such as seating arrangements, and content should reflect the equal opportunities policy of the school. For some children worship might be a totally alien concept and some may be openly hostile to it. Care is needed to provide a positive atmosphere for these children. The right of parents to withdraw their children is upheld by law, but suitable provision should be made for those children who will not attend.

Monitoring assembly

Head teachers are responsible for ensuring that regular worship takes place in their school. Many find that keeping records of assemblies helps to establish patterns and monitor content. Records can be useful in helping staff to plan, particularly from year to year. They can also be extremely useful to show other interested parties what kind of worship is going on in their school particularly in relation to the 1988 Act. Besides keeping a record of the content and features of each assembly, it is helpful for monitoring purposes to note particular pros and cons which can be taken into account when a similar assembly is organised again.

Planning the assembly

Thus we come to planning the individual assembly. The weekly theme is chosen and the teacher must now plan for the particular day. The planning which takes place is very similar to the way many teachers plan their lessons. Based on the weekly theme and other considerations, e.g. curriculum, the teacher will decide on the topic for the assembly. Next she will consider the children for whom it is planned. Their ages, aptitudes, previous knowledge, religious backgrounds will help to focus on the content. The teacher needs to be quite sure what the main aim of the assembly is and select her material appropriately. The presentation will depend upon the nature of the content, resources, the number of children and the time allocated. Also to be considered is how far the concept of 'worship' has been built into the assembly and whether the assembly is part of the 'broadly Christian' acts of worship or not.

It is important at this stage to reflect on the difference between the words 'assembly' and 'worship'. Assembly is the term the staff and children will use to describe the activity. But an assembly need not involve 'worship', which, for this to be achieved, needs to be positively built into the planning. Giving out notices and reporting on match results is not worship. If these things are to be included in assembly time they should not be allowed to interrupt the worship element. Traditionally these things are saved till after the worship but this hardly encourages the children to carry away with them the thoughts of that part of the assembly. Perhaps the notices should be given out first. Throughout this chapter we have emphasised the need for assemblies to be properly prepared. The following questions may serve as a checklist in planning an act of worship.

Beginning of assembly: How will the atmosphere be set? Will there be quietness? music? singing? How will the topic be introduced? Will it be explicitly linked to the rest of the school curriculum, perhaps to some topic work?

Middle of assembly: Is there to be a worship element? Is the material suitable for the age range? What will be the main method of presentation?

End of assembly: How will it conclude? Is there a place for a 'prayer-like' activity? Will there be any follow-up work in the classroom? Will it lead on to another assembly?

Conclusion

The main concern of this chapter has been to answer the question, '*How* do we do assemblies?' The suggestions put forward have sought to present ways of ensuring that collective worship is a regular, interesting and purposeful part of the school day. Such provision calls for a concerted effort on the part of everyone in the school, requiring time and sufficient planning of the kind used in other curriculum areas.

CHAPTER 6
Collective Worship for Infants

We are going to have a prayer. Let us kneel everyone.
'Thy art father that sang and save thy all night and said until Thee faithful what
ye faith unto me:
I say unto you and you say unto me:
the Holy Ghost and the medical workers.'
Will you say after me please:
'Thy deliberately faith I full
Faith against almighty worship God,
and faith all unto you
Faith against thy holy prayer.'

This passage was part of a tape recording of a six year old playing at
assembly. The whole passage can be found in Mumford (1982), but
was originally part of Ronald Goldman's research into children's
understanding of religion (Goldman, 1965). Mumford records how the
child spoke in a 'holy voice', demonstrating how he was becoming
aware of the 'specialness' of the act of worship. Mumford argues that
while the words have no literal meaning, the passage shows a
developing awareness 'that what is happening is important to adults
whom he loves and who love him' (pp48-9).

The passage clearly illustrates the need to give careful consideration
to the content of infant assemblies. If collective worship is to be seen as
a valuable educational activity, it must be planned with the children's
levels of understanding in mind. We would not wish to give them
something which is too complex to be meaningful nor something
which compromises the children's religious or non-religious backgrounds. Instead we should be planning activities which clearly
attempt to achieve the purposes identified by the school.

To consider the role of collective worship in the infant school it is
first necessary to go back to the requirements of the 1988 Education

Reform Act to identify what is required by law. From here we can begin to build a picture of what is appropriate to children in their earliest years of schooling.

Developing the spiritual, moral and cultural

The statutory requirement to develop children's spiritual, moral and cultural understanding is a basic requirement of the curriculum in all schools. It has been shown elsewhere in this book that collective worship can contribute to this development. Worship should be seen as an integral part of the children's religious education and so the guidelines for religious education produced by the local authorities will be of value here.

The 1988 Act does not set any age limits to its requirements regarding school worship, and so we must assume that spiritual, moral and cultural development begins as soon as the child enters school. The task here is to identify how that can best be done with the youngest children. Further examination of the 1988 Act reveals certain factors which the legislators took to be important.

Consideration of family background

It is made clear in the Act that the family backgrounds of the children must be taken into account. This is important when considering young children who may not have developed ideas of what their family background is. Those children who have a religious background may be familiar with forms of worship as they take place in the home and place of worship. They may be used to taking part in worship either in words or actions, and may certainly have watched adults doing so. They may have a religious vocabulary and have begun to develop their own understanding of terms such as 'God' and 'prayer'. They may have a knowledge of some religious literature and stories and have experienced religious ceremonies and festivals. At the same time they are not likely to have a sophisticated view of the beliefs of their religion, and they are not likely to recognise when an activity in assembly runs contrary to their family's beliefs.

Children from non-religious backgrounds may find the language and concepts of worship totally alien. Indeed, for many children, school assembly will be the first time they encounter worship. This too needs to be taken into account, and we must avoid making assumptions about children's religious knowledge and beliefs.

First of all, it is essential that we make children aware of their role in assemblies. Young children soon become 'institutionalised' in our schools. One only has to observe the nursery children joining the rest of the school in assembly to see how quickly they conform to the requirements of school, and sit in rows quietly and attentively. Children soon get used to doing as they are told and expecting the teacher to give them instructions. In such a climate it is easy to have the children 'put their hands together and close their eyes to pray'. All the same, we must ensure that the activities we plan for assembly do not involve the children in doing anything which they or their families would be uncomfortable with.

The key word in the Warwickshire guide (1989) is *sensitivity*:

> This will ensure the use of material in songs, meditations and prayers which does not give offence, and forms of words which invite, rather than demand, participation, allowing all children to feel at one with those around them and to respond as seems most natural to them. (p16)

This emphasis on choosing material to which all pupils can relate, places a good deal of responsibility on teachers to acquaint themselves with the practices of the different traditions within the school. Books such as David Rose's *Home, School and Faith* (1992) give good guidelines on some of the traditions followed by children in our schools.

Consideration of ages and abilities

For infant teachers, the need to provide for the children's immaturity, is probably the most demanding aspect of assembly. Worship is essentially an adult occupation and so ways must be found to take into account the level of development of the children in order to comply with the 1988 Act. Too often in primary schools the activities which take place in assembly bear no relation to the work which is done in lesson time. The value of play, experiential learning, concrete experiences, child centredness, which have influenced young children's education for decades, often find no place in the assembly.

Good assemblies are those which utilise such approaches to teaching and learning. We should expect to see children actively learning through assemblies, with use made of the materials and resources considered vital in the classroom. Account must also be taken of children with specific learning difficulties.

A major impact on the teaching of religious education in this country has been the work of Ronald Goldman in the 1960s. Although his work was developed essentially from a Christian standpoint and has been challenged in later years (see Bastide, 1987), many of his findings have direct relevance for collective worship. Working on a framework similar to Piaget's theories of cognitive development, Goldman identified a series of stages which he believed characterised children's religious development, descriptions of which can be found in his books *Readiness for Religion* (1965) and *Religious Thinking from Childhood to Adolescence* (1964).

Essentially the theory is expounded that children in the earliest years of education are unable to understand many religious concepts. Goldman argued that adult forms and expressions of worship were totally inappropriate for use with young children. He therefore advocated a re-thinking of worship through the eyes and experiences of children: 'The heart of the matter is that worship for the young child must be at a personal, immediate level of experience if it is to be real' (1965, p96).

This theory has led to an emphasis on an 'implicit' approach to young children's religious education. This means that in many acts of worship the religious content will be 'implied' and will be concerned with what Mumford (1982) calls, 'laying foundations' for an understanding of worship rather than involving the use of explicitly religious material.

The emphasis on starting with the children's experiences can be seen in the most valuable assemblies. Such topics as families, homes, myself, are thus considered appropriate starting points. There is, however, the danger that such assemblies can become restricted to the little world of the infant school, and so attempts should be made to draw on material of a wider nature. This is not difficult to do in our society which contains so many cultures and has access to the world through travel and television. Even so, at the centre must lie the question, 'What does worship mean to young children?' As Goldman said, it should be examined through their eyes rather than through ours.

Hull (1975) also questions the ability of children to understand the term worship as adults understand it. He maintains that young children in particular may be unable to worship due to their inability to comprehend the beliefs upon which worship is based. Unlike Goldman, Hull does not see it as part of the school's role to induct children into Christianity. Whereas Goldman would see 'implicit worship' as a foundation for Christian worship in the fullest sense of the term, Hull argues that the aim should be to bring children only to the 'threshold of worship'. It is not the school's responsibility to demand that the children cross this threshold. Children are thus introduced to activities which may give them some understanding of worship, but do not demand that they worship as such.

The difference between the work of Goldman and Hull lies in their intentions. The former sees worship as part of Christian education; the latter's approach is not tied to any specific faith. In a state primary school it is Hull's standpoint which is going to be the most appropriate. However, both writers suggest that there is a need to think very carefully about the aims and content of assemblies. A list of questions may help to identify those considerations which should be made when planning:

- Does the assembly contribute to the children's religious education?
- Are the children aware of their role in assembly?
- Is the language and material appropriate to their ages and abilities?
- Are the concepts appropriate to their ages and abilities?

If the answers to these questions are 'Yes' then the teacher can feel confident that she is going some way to present worship which is educationally valuable.

The aims and content of infant worship

In this section an attempt will be made to show how worship can be planned by taking into account the legal, practical and educational considerations. In planning assemblies, the teacher should have in mind:

- the terms of the 1988 Act;
- LEA guidelines;
- school policy;
- resources available;
- appropriate teaching and learning methods.

Suggested aims for infant assembly

Collective worship should provide opportunities for the children to:

- recognise their own value as individuals;
- recognise their own feelings and responses to people and situations;
- reflect on their relationships with others;
- develop empathy for other people;
- reflect on the awe and wonder of the world they live in;

- recognise their own responsibilities for themselves and their world;
- begin to recognise that some questions are unanswerable;
- begin to recognise that some people have a religious view of life;
- share in the special occasions and festivals of different cultures and traditions.

What follows is an example of how infant assemblies might be planned across a year. Half-termly themes are taken from those typical in an infant curriculum, providing for children to the top of Key Stage One, with the weekly assembly themes (column 3) making an integral contribution. In the remainder of the chapter, one of the themes is explored.

	HALF-TERMLY SCHOOL THEMES	WEEKLY ASSEMBLY THEMES
AUTUMN TERM	Myself	Birthdays
		Beginnings
		Children
		Caring
		Memories
		Happiness
	Change	Autumn
		Harvest
		Day and night
		Time
		Decisions
		Good and evil
		Divali
SPRING TERM	Families	Love and hate
		Precious things
		Sharing
		Responsibility
		Old age
		Special times
	New life	A new baby
		The Earth
		Beauty
		Patterns
		New from old
		Passover
		Easter
SUMMER TERM	People	Achievement

People who help us
People in our school
Courage
Strangers
In others' shoes
Water   Value and worth
Journeys
Water life
Rain
Pollution
Baptism

Example of a week's assemblies on precious things

We now focus on one of the assembly themes for the spring term, 'precious things', and consider how the week's assemblies might be planned. In each assembly description which follows, the main aim and content is given. No songs or prayers are included, as these would be chosen in keeping with the school's policy. Considerations regarding the setting, atmosphere, the use of music and so on will also need to be considered.

Overall aim: to encourage children to reflect on things which are precious to the individual and to the whole of humankind.

DAY ONE: whole-school assembly.   LEADER: a teacher.

Objective: to help children begin to recognise that some things are precious only to individuals.

Preparation: obtain a copy of the story *Dogger* by Shirley Hughes (1979, Picture Lions).

Display the word 'Precious' in large letters.

1. Ask the children if anyone can read the word that is displayed. Then ask if anyone knows what it means or what things they know are precious. From this it can be established if children know the word and what they understand by it. Points to raise are: precious means personally valuable or special but not necessarily expensive; some precious things are worth a lot of money, some precious things are not.

2. Introduce the story as one which tells of a precious thing which is not worth a lot of money. Read or tell the story all the way through. At the end ask questions bringing out the preciousness of Dogger, e.g.

What thing was precious to the little boy?
How do we know it was precious to him?
Why do you think it was precious to him?
Was Dogger worth a lot of money?
Was Dogger precious to anyone else?
Why didn't the boy just get another toy?

3. In a moment of quietness ask the children to think about what things are precious to them.
4. Ask the children to tell you of things they have which are precious to them. Encourage them to say why they are precious.

DAY TWO: class assembly.　　LEADER: the class teacher.
Objective:　to help children reflect further on things which are precious to other people.
Preparation: a) teacher brings something precious to school;
　　　　　　b) either, ask the children to bring their precious things into school,
　　　　　　or have the children draw/paint pictures of their precious things.

1. Show the children the object which is precious to you and explain why. Invite the children to show each other their precious things and explain why they are precious.
2. Explain to the children that many things are precious because of the people or time they remind us of. Ask the children if their precious objects remind them of something or someone if this has not already come out.
3. Tell the children that if anyone mistreated or took your special object you would be very upset. Encourage the children to discuss treatment of others' precious things by asking questions such as:

How would you feel if someone mistreated your precious thing?
How should we treat other people's precious things?

4. Ask the children to close their eyes and think about the words you are about to say.

Some things are very precious to us and we like to keep them safe. We must remember that different things are precious to other people and we must try to treat their precious things properly too.

N.B. Some children may bring in religious objects and care will have to be taken about how these objects are stored and treated.

DAY THREE: year group assembly.   LEADER: a parent.
Objective: to help children begin to recognise that people are precious.
Preparation: ask a parent to come and talk to the children about why her/ his children are precious to them.

1. Remind children of the theme for the week and ask them to recap on the issues which have been raised. Introduce the parent, and tell them that he/she is going to talk about what is precious to them – and it's not an object.
2. The parent might wish to tell stories about their children, show photographs, bring their children in etc. The main point should be that her/his children are very precious to them – even when they are naughty, and that they try to keep them safe.
3. Children should spend some moments reflecting on the people who are precious to them. They might wish to identify parents, friends, relatives, brothers and sisters, etc.

DAY FOUR: class assembly.   LEADER: a teacher.
Objective: to help children begin to recognise that the Earth is precious.
Preparation: a) obtain a globe or map of the world. This assembly would be extra effective if it took place outside so that children are more aware of the world around them.
          b) board or sheet of paper for writing a list.

1. Have the globe or map covered, and ask the children to guess what precious thing is underneath. When it is revealed make it clear to the children that it is not the map or globe itself but the Earth that is precious.
2. Discuss why the Earth is precious. Ask questions such as:

Why is the Earth precious?
What precious things are on it?
Why is it precious to humans/animals/plants?

3. Move the discussion on to the treatment of the Earth by reminding the children that we treat precious things with care. Ask questions such as:

Who is the Earth precious to?

We take care of our precious things, who takes care of the Earth?
How can we take care of the Earth?
What things could each one of us do?

Write up answers on the board or sheet.

4. Have a moment of silent thought. If the assembly is outside, this could be done lying down looking up at the sky, or in a circle holding hands.

Follow up: Children could write poems or prose, draw or paint about the precious Earth.

DAY FIVE: whole school.   LEADER: a pupil with other children.
Objective: to enable children to share their learning of the week on precious things.
Preparation: collect samples from classes of work on precious things. Prepare older children for announcing the assembly and asking children to show their work.

1. The pupil tells the other children that today they are going to share their thoughts on precious things. He/she uses a prepared list to ask different children to stand and share their work.
2. CONCLUSION: the leader asks the children to close their eyes and listen to some words:

This week we have been thinking of precious things.
We have looked at precious objects.
We have remembered special people.
We have thought of the precious Earth on which we live.
We know that precious things need taking care of.
And now we have shared a precious moment enjoying each other's work.

(The children could join in and repeat each line.)

Summary of the week

It is best if the assemblies for the week are closely built around one theme and begin with the children's own experiences before considering others' and eventually a global view. Each assembly is organised in a different way, offering variety of leader, presentation, setting and content. This prevents assembly becoming predictable and routine. Use is made of children's experiences, and the content and style of presentation is clearly aimed at the ages of the pupils involved. Home/school links are included with an assembly led by a parent. Children's conceptual understanding is broadened by encouraging them to think of a variety of uses of the word 'precious'.

The assemblies contain 'implicit' religious material, appropriate for the age range, but there is the possibility of explicit material being incorporated, for example, religious artefacts or holy books. Schools might feel that there are some religious stories which would be appropriate for inclusion.

The assemblies are of value both to children's religious education and to their wider development and would form part of sound foundational learning essential to their understanding of worship and religion.

Conclusion

In this chapter the focus has been how to plan assemblies with infants in mind. It has been shown that there are specific requirements for effective collective worship with young children. It will not do to present children with a 'mini-service' based upon adult lines. Instead the approaches, methods and content of good infant teaching and learning must be utilised in order to make assembly time a special and valuable learning experience for all children.

CHAPTER 7
Collective Worship for Juniors

The junior years in school represent a significant time for children's experiences of collective worship. The development and maturation of children during this period means that we have to be keenly aware of how they are interpreting and understanding worship. Too often children can be alienated from worship because of their experiences of poor assemblies at this age. Some of the older children I spoke to in my study spoke of assemblies being boring and lasting too long. Some saw it simply as a time when teachers could be freed to do other work.

In order to provide assemblies which hold the attention of older children and offer them something meaningful, certain factors should be considered. Firstly, it must be remembered that children at Key Stage Two, or the junior years, will already have been in school for up to three years. In three years of assemblies they may have encountered teachers' favourite stories several times. There is the danger that they may see some stories as babyish because they know they had them in the infants. Any point being raised may then be lost as the children switch off. This is particularly important with regard to religious stories. By the time children reach the top of the junior age range they may have heard some Bible stories many times. Of course there is value in the repetition of favourite stories and of coming to them again with a maturer outlook, but again we would wish to avoid junior pupils coming to the conclusion that the Bible is only a book for young children.

A second factor to consider is the moral and behavioural aspect of assembly. Because assembly is one of the few times when schools gather together, there is the temptation to use the occasion to reprimand children or tell them how they should behave. This may have a variety of adverse effects. Children may see religion as nothing more than a set of rules and regulations and assembly as the time when the head tells them off. Moreover, if moral behaviour is seen as solely

linked to assembly and religion, then children may draw the conclusion that only religious people are moral.

These two factors, the purpose and content of assembly, are
probably the most significant in alienating children from the concept
of worship. A further factor which may contribute is that older
children will be much more aware of teacher attitudes. If they
recognise that teachers are participating in worship reluctantly, they
too will begin to class it as a nuisance which interrupts the school day.
I recall many children who, at the prospect of assembly, would
graciously offer to clean cupboards, take the register to the secretary,
water the plants . . .

How then do we provide collective worship for older primary
children which is both educative and enjoyable? We shall begin by
looking at some of the characteristics of upper primary children and
some of the features of their curriculum.

Religious development in the junior years

When Ronald Goldman (1964) researched the religious development
of children, he identified three levels of development. He described
children of the mental age of between seven and eleven as being at
either the intuitive or concrete stages of religious thought. By this he
meant that certain abstract religious concepts are interpreted in
concrete terms by children in order to make them meaningful. For
example, he says that children at this stage have a concept of God
which is dominated by the image of a huge man in Palestinian clothes,
the Bible is seen as book of magic which is totally true and prayer is
something you do when you want some material possession. Goldman
postulated that because of their abstract nature, many religious
concepts were beyond the understanding of junior children, and
argued that they should not therefore be introduced to them until the
latter end of the junior phase, i.e. at about the age of eleven.

Dennis Bates (in Bastide, 1992), however, in tracing the development of ideas on children's thinking since Goldman, finds that current
thinking allows for the possibility that children are much more capable
of understanding abstract concepts than previously thought. As a
result more 'explicitly' religious themes now legitimately form a
greater part of children's religious curriculum than they did previously. Within this context it seems appropriate that collective
worship for junior children will incorporate use of religious material
and concepts, reflecting a growing awareness in children of the place
of religion in people's lives.

If children are growing up in a religious tradition at home then they may already have detailed knowledge, skills and understandings of religious ritual and belief by the time they reach the junior years. They may already be taking part in rites of passage through which they are becoming adult members of the faith. For example, Roman Catholic children may at the age of seven take their first Holy Communion, which marks a transitional stage in their religious development. More generally, many children will have experienced religious ceremonies such as marriage, where they may have been bridesmaids or page boys. They may also have taken part in festivals and have begun to take an active part in services. In many religious traditions, children will be attending 'Sunday school' or the equivalent, in which they may be learning more about the history and beliefs of their religion. They may even be learning other languages: Jewish children may be learning Hebrew, Muslim children Arabic, and so on.

Children from no religious tradition will also be building their own picture of what religion is all about. There will be some from nominally Christian backgrounds who are very familiar with Christian festivals and traditions of marriage etc, while those from all back-grounds cannot fail to notice Christmas and Easter, and may have seen television services based on Christian tradition. Children will also be aware of the different religious traditions among pupils and staff in their school and neighbourhood. Through the medium of television, they may even be aware of different religions across the world. They will be starting to build pictures in their minds about what it means to be a Christian as distinct from, say, a Muslim or Sikh.

Children from religious and non-religious backgrounds alike, may also be starting to build stereotypical images of different religious groups. It is up to teachers to ensure that assemblies do not reinforce these stereotypes. Some children may be developing an intolerance of religion or particular religions because of what they hear outside school, and this too must be addressed within the assembly. Finally, there may be children who are being brought up in a very strict tradition who are beginning to rebel. These children may be develop-ing a hostility to their own or any religion and may 'switch off' in assembly in response to this.

What we begin to see in the junior years, then, is a picture of children who are beginning their own search into the world of religion. They will have a certain amount of knowledge gleaned from home, school and their environment, they will be starting to wrestle with religious concepts, and they will be starting to consider what impact those religious concepts have in their own lives. This is why in many religious education syllabuses, children of junior age are introduced to a more explicit approach to religion than infant children. Specific religious topics and traditions are introduced, and artefacts, books, visits are utilised, with children often asked to contribute from their own experiences and knowledge. All these features need to be used in the assemblies planned for this age group.

Of course, children at this stage are not only developing religiously, but are also developing in a variety of ways, physically, emotionally and intellectually. We will now explore these other areas of development to see if here too there are implications for the planning of collective worship.

Other characteristics of junior children

Children at Key Stage Two are beginning to possess knowledge, skills and concepts which enable them to become much more independent in their learning. They are becoming skilled readers and writers, and developing their skills in oral communication, organisation, reflection, presentation, reasoning and so on. All of these should be focused upon in assemblies.

Liz Collis (in Bastide, 1992) recognises the value of collective worship in developing many of these skills, particularly in communication: 'How children show what they have been learning about to others reinforces the child's own learning, develops communication skills and celebrates the child's work and achievement' (p48). She adds that this also contributes to the learning experiences of the audience. Children at this stage are becoming increasingly concerned with the attitudes and behaviour of their peers, and respond well to assemblies presented by other children. Children at the junior stage are also becoming used to working independently and in groups. These two learning methods can be effectively employed in assembly.

Children's moral development at this stage is also significant for collective worship. We have seen that children quickly recognise when assembly is being used as a vehicle for moral teaching, since it is an area which is increasingly significant in their lives. Junior children are becoming aware of rules, both in their own games and in relation to behaviour. They are learning what is acceptable to adults, to the school and to society. While morality is obviously something which will often find its way into collective worship, teachers should be aware of the dangers of relating moral behaviour solely to religion. Issues of right and wrong are complex, and we should avoid imposing on children a set of standards, on the grounds that they can be justified only in terms of religious beliefs, which they may ultimately reject. This would not only be conceptually misleading, but would leave the children impoverished with no strategies for developing their own guidelines for behaviour. There would be something tragic in a child's religious education if they should be left with the question, 'I don't believe in God, therefore why should I be good?'

Collective worship and the junior curriculum

The National Curriculum has put emphasis on the discreteness of the different subject areas in order to ensure that children cover all the necessary subjects adequately. In many schools, however, there has been a retention of a topic-based approach for two reasons. Firstly, schools are concerned that the amount of time in a school day does not allow for separate timetabling of the different subjects. Secondly, it is recognised that such segregation may not be beneficial to young children's education. In their search for meaning, it is believed, children do not see the world in terms of discrete subject areas. It was recognised by Goldman (1965) that to separate religious education from the rest of the curriculum made religion seem alien and different and not connected to everyday life. Liz Collis (in Bastide, 1992) also recognises the value of incorporating religion into topic themes. She finds that subjects inform each other and that religious education needs the other subjects as vehicles for its expression. On this argument, collective worship, as part of religious education, is best linked to the general work of the school. It is suggested that the content for collective worship is thus best found in both the children's own experiences, and the work they do in the classroom.

In recent years, however, the topic approach to the curriculum has been criticised, not least for the artificial nature of the links sometimes made between subject areas. An examination of some of those which have been drawn for religious education illustrates this danger; tenuous links based on topics such as 'transport' or 'materials' do nothing to advance the cause of the topic approach. The Government commissioned report by Alexander *et al.* (1992) highlighted the possible short-comings of 'broad-based' topics, maintaining that they often led to inadequate coverage of curriculum areas due to a lack of focus. The report also criticised 'non-differentiation' whereby the distinctiveness of curriculum areas in topic work is denied. Instead, the use of 'integration' is preferred, which brings subjects together, while recognising their uniqueness. The report goes on to suggest that there is value in the topic approach when it is handled carefully, and recommends 'subject-focused' topics, in which one subject area is central, as the best choice. With this in mind, it is clear that there will be occasions when the work of the classroom does not relate directly to worship, and on these occasions the seasons, festivals and current events are more likely to offer suitable subject matter for assemblies. However, during the course of the year there will be ample opportunity to explore at least some classroom topics in assembly.

Indeed, assembly time may be an ideal opportunity to cover some aspects of the National Curriculum. Palmer and Breuilly (1992) illustrate how this might be done when they outline some assemblies which would relate to the programmes of study in history. For example, their assembly 'Open the prison gates' is linked to core study unit 2, Tudors and Stuarts, and asks the children to reflect on the plight of people imprisoned on political grounds.

In considering the characteristics of junior children and their curriculum, it can be seen that we are addressing the main requirements of the 1988 Act regarding collective worship. The Act demands that the family backgrounds, ages and abilities of the children should be taken into account. What we have done here is to focus specifically on this age group to examine exactly what it means to take these things into account. In the following section there will be some examples of how these considerations are put into practice. The main guiding principles for selection of aims and content are:

- children's religious development;
- the requirements of the 1988 Act;
- the requirements of the National Curriculum;
- themes commonly found in the junior curriculum.

Suggested aims for junior assemblies

Collective worship should offer children opportunities to:

- reflect on their value as individuals;
- recognise their responsibilities to themselves and their world;
- reflect on the awe and wonder of the world;
- develop empathy with others;
- begin to find their own answers to life's 'ultimate questions', e.g. Why am I here? What happens after death?;
- recognise that individuals' actions are determined by their beliefs;
- recognise the religious response to ultimate questions;

80

- begin to appreciate the significance of sacred writings, symbols and rituals in the lives of believers;
- participate in the sharing of festive and memorable occasions from various cultures and traditions.

An example of yearly planning for collective worship

Below is an example of how assemblies can be planned across the year, based upon the themes being followed by the school in its general curriculum work. Some themes are drawn from the calendar, and while most are initially 'implicit' in nature (see Chapter 6 for definition), there is ample scope for development into more 'explicit' content.

	HALF-TERMLY SCHOOL THEMES	WEEKLY ASSEMBLY THEMES
AUTUMN	Community	Belonging
		Buildings
		Our neighbourhood
		Our country
		Our world
		Our religions
	Signs and symbols	Sign posts
		Light
		Religious dress
		Religious objects
		Hanukah
		Christmas
SPRING	Communication	Science
		Messages
		Sight and blindness
		Language
		Feelings
		Films
	The past	Something old
		Grandparents
		Heroes
		Religious leaders
		Events
		Time
SUMMER	Buildings	Windows

Achievement
Challenge
Pilgrimage
Places of worship
Worship at home

Books   Stories
Information
Journeys
Words
Diaries
Holy books

Below is an example of how one of these themes could be developed to provide for a week of assemblies. The assemblies are outlined with several thoughts in mind. First is consideration of the age and background of the children. The intended audience is seven to eleven years old, multi-faith and with some knowledge of religious topics. The aim is to provide for assemblies for different size groups, involving a variety of leaders, and keeping the children as actively involved as possible.

A week's assemblies on the theme of heroes/heroines

MAIN AIMS: to help children understand the use of the term 'Heroes' and various qualities which heroes can have. To help children develop a broad understanding of who can be a hero or heroine without being restricted to stereotypes.

DAY ONE: whole school.   LEADER: a teacher.

Objective: to help children reflect on their understanding of the word 'hero'.

Preparation: obtain video extract about a cartoon hero, e.g. Danger Mouse, Captain Planet, Teenage Mutant Hero Turtles, or whoever is popular at the time. A large sheet of paper or writing board.

1. Without introduction, show a piece of the film. It need only be brief, but should contain a scene in which the hero is displaying his/her skills.
2. Begin discussion about the hero's qualities to bring out the theme. Use questions such as:

   - Who is this character and is he/she real?
   - What happens in their programme?

82

- Who do they fight against?
- Are they good or bad? Why?
- What special powers do they have?
- Would they be called a hero? Why?

3. Develop the discussion into a general one about the meaning of 'hero'. Use questions such as:

- What do we mean when we call someone a hero?
- What skills would they have?
- Do they have to be strong, clever, brave?
- Do they have to be famous?

4. A list can be made on the paper of qualities which the children think heroes should have. Encourage the children to think of specific incidences of heroism or specific people, famous and not. Require the children to explain why these people are heroes and encourage them to challenge each other if they disagree.
5. End the assembly by asking the children in a moment of quietness to think about people whom they think of as heroes.

DAY TWO: year groups.   LEADER: a teacher.

Objective: to help children recognise that a hero may defeat personal disabilities.

Preparation: find a story about a famous person who overcame physical difficulties, e.g. Stevie Wonder (in *Hand in Hand Assembly Book* by Proffitt and Bishop, 1983)

1. Ask the children to recall the content of yesterday's assembly and what they learned. Tell them they will hear a story about someone who was a hero, Stevie Wonder.
2. Read or tell the story and then ask the children questions about why Stevie could be considered a hero. Bring out issues related to overcoming disability, using personal talents, giving happiness to others etc.
3. Play some of Stevie Wonder's music. (If another person is used, show something of their achievements.)
4. Ask the children to close their eyes and listen while you read some words, e.g.

We don't need to be extra strong to be a hero,
We don't need to climb the tallest mountain,
    or fight terrible monsters.
To be a hero we need to take the gifts we have

And use them wisely, with all our strength
and courage.

Follow up: children do a short piece of writing on someone they
consider to be a hero, explaining why.

DAY THREE: class assembly.   LEADER: the children.

Objective: to help children identify those people they consider to be
heroes, and why.
Preparation: in the classroom, children do some of their own writing
about their own hero. The teacher does the same.

1. Have the children come to the assembly with their piece of
   writing. Tell them they are going to share their heroes. The
   teacher begins by reading a short passage about her own hero.
   Ideally the teacher should write honestly about her hero, but if
   ideas are not forthcoming, some good examples can be found
   in assembly books e.g. *Activity Assemblies for Christian Collective Worship* by Elizabeth Peirce (1991).
2. Children volunteer to read out their own writing. Encourage
   them to explain what qualities their hero has.
3. In a moment of quietness the children reflect on what they
   have heard in the assembly.

DAY FOUR: year group.   LEADER: a local religious leader.

Objective: to introduce the children to a personality from a
religious tradition who is considered to be a hero.
Preparation: contact a local priest, Rabbi, Imam etc and ask him/
her to tell the story of someone who is considered a
hero in his faith. It need not be a scriptural character, it
could be a modern-day hero.

1. Introduce the leader and explain that he/she is going to tell
   them about a hero of their faith.
2. At the end of the narration, encourage the children to ask
   questions about what they have heard.
3. Ask the leader to say a prayer from their tradition to finish the
   assembly. The children should be asked to close their eyes or
   listen very carefully.

DAY FIVE: whole school.   LEADER: the children.

Objective: to encourage the children to recognise that even
children can be heroes.

Preparation: This assembly can be used as a time to share the achievements of individual children with the whole school. Certificates for sport, music, Brownie badges and other out of school endeavours can be brought in and displayed.

Older children in the school should prepare the assembly by collecting information from books, television, newspapers about children who have shown heroic qualities.

1. Children introduce assembly and explain that being a hero is to do with endeavour, courage, perseverance and thought for others. Also, that anyone can be a hero, at any age.
2. Some examples can then be shown either in pictures or on film. There may even be children in the school who could be considered to be heroes in their own way.
3. Conclude with a passage for reflection written by the children.

Stories of heroes: resources

Hand in Hand Assembly Book
Russell Proffitt and Valerie Bishop
Longman (1983)

Ottobah Cugoano
Scott Joplin
Rosa Parks
Muhammad Ali
Bob Marley
Mary Seacole
Mahatma Ghandi
Marcus Garvey
Sybil Phoenix
Martin Luther King
Alexander Dumas

Activity Assemblies for Christian Collective Worship 5-11
Elizabeth Peirce
Falmer (1991)

Gideon
St Francis of Assissi
Grace Darling
St Paul
Elijah
St Margaret

Activity Assemblies for Multi-racial Schools 5-11
Elizabeth Peirce
Falmer (1992)

Abraham
Muhammad (pbuh)
Siddhartha
Gautama
Guru Nanak

Conclusion

The purpose of this chapter has been to identify the special requirements of collective worship for older primary children. It can be seen
that it is necessary to take into account the increasing maturity of the
children to provide worship that is effective and valuable. Children of
junior age are more likely to have some understanding of religious
issues than their younger school mates. They are beginning to try to
make sense of their world by piecing together what they learn from
home, from school, from their friends, from their religion, from the
television and what they know from themselves.

The purpose of collective worship at this stage is to help them in this
quest for understanding. Schools need to provide a rich and varied
diet in assemblies with material drawn from the world's religious and
non-religious life stances, so that they can begin to identify their place
and role in the world at large. In this way, collective worship can make
a valid contribution to the spiritual, moral and cultural development
of the children, enabling children to become truly 'religiate'.

CHAPTER 8
Resources for Worship

Introduction

The requirements to provide collective worship every day in schools makes great demands on resources. At the same time there is great competition for resources in school and often collective worship may be low on the list of priorities. The purpose of this chapter is primarily to demonstrate that resourcing assembly need not be time-consuming or expensive. Many items and materials which are readily available in the primary school make excellent resources for RE. Not only do these provide a cheap way of funding assembly but they also provide links between worship and the rest of the curriculum. Besides items and materials, there is also a wealth of literature specifically designed for worship from which a school can select.

It is essential for teachers to be creative when resourcing worship. First of all it is necessary to provide variety for the children to help them become aware of diversity in worship. Although teachers may long for 'one book' from which they can take all their assemblies, such an approach might give children a misleading impression of what worship should be like. It would result in a concentration on the particular choices made by the writer, and it might suggest to children that assembly is just to do with that particular book. It could also result in a complacency on the part of the children as they are presented with assemblies which are similar in tone and presentation.

A variety of resources ensures not only that justice is given to different faith stances, but also that religious concepts are each presented in a variety of ways. It also provides teachers who are nervous about assembly with a range of material from which they can choose and which they can be sure does not compromise their own beliefs.

In the section below, a wide range of resources for worship are suggested. Some items and materials are typically available in schools and require no special investment for the purposes of assembly, while others are particularly designed for worship. Also, some are primarily for the teachers' use, while others are appropriate for children to use.

Materials are listed under the following headings:

- Artefacts and natural objects
- People
- Food
- Audio-visual materials
- Teachers' books
- Books for children

Artefacts and natural objects

Using artefacts and other objects in assembly is an excellent way of presenting material. They provide a sensual aspect to the activity, offering opportunity for seeing, smelling, touching or hearing. In providing something concrete to see, artefacts can focus children's attention and stimulate their interest, enabling them to concentrate on the theme being presented.

It is essential to remember that the larger the group of children, the larger the artefact must be. There is little value in holding up an intricately carved and tiny rosary which only the front row can properly discern. It is also important to remember that some religious artefacts must be treated with particular respect. All religious objects should be treated carefully, and part of the children's learning will be to develop respect for those things which are sacred to someone else. Care must be taken to observe any rituals associated with particular objects, such as washing before touching holy books. Further guidelines on this can be found in *Good Practice in Primary Religious Education 4–11* by D. Bastide (1992, p138).

Some schools keep collections of artefacts as part of their RE resources, and these can obviously be a valuable source of material for worship. Many religious objects can be found in shops in areas where there are communities of particular religious traditions. For example, greetings cards for Divali, Eid and Bar-Mitzvah, are readily available in many localities within larger cities.

When using artefacts it is necessary to be quite clear about your purpose in showing it. Barnett (in Bastide, 1992) emphasises the fact that children should be encouraged to reflect on the significance of the object, because 'the artefact which is merely described and copied remains an empty vessel, relevant only for others, soon forgotten' (p133). Instead, children should be asked to evaluate the significance of the object for believers, reflect on the impact it makes on peoples' lives, relate the object to their own experience, and so on. There are a variety of purposes for which an artefact may be used. Among these are:

- To show something which is used at a special time, e.g. birth certificate, Divali lamp.
- To show the symbolic use of the object, e.g. candle, prayer shawl, turban.
- To illustrate a theme e.g. precious things, happy times, journeys.

Figure 8.1 shows two examples of how an artefact can be used in each of these respects.

Religious artefacts include:

Christianity –	Bible	Hinduism–	Puja tray
	Rosary		Statues of deities
	Cross		Divali lamp
	Baptism certificate		Garlands
	Candle		
	Advent calendar		
	Palm cross	Islam –	Qu'ran stand
			Prayer beads
Judaism –	Prayer shawl		Prayer mat
	Mezuzah		Compass
	Passover plate		Festival cards
	Cappel		
Sikhism –	Turban	Buddhism –	Statues
	Five 'K's		Pictures
	Jewellery		

Natural and other objects

There are many objects which are not religious but which nevertheless provide effective starting points for assembly. The list is endless, but below are some items which have proved particularly useful:

A decorated box	Clothes
A glass of water	A bowl
An apple	A shell

a) A candle:

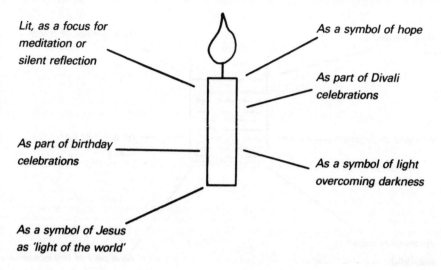

Lit, as a focus for meditation or silent reflection

As a symbol of hope

As part of Divali celebrations

As part of birthday celebrations

As a symbol of light overcoming darkness

As a symbol of Jesus as 'light of the world'

b) Festival cards:

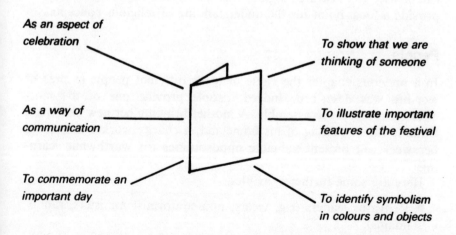

As an aspect of celebration

To show that we are thinking of someone

As a way of communication

To illustrate important features of the festival

To commemorate an important day

To identify symbolism in colours and objects

Fig. 8.1

A glass of water:

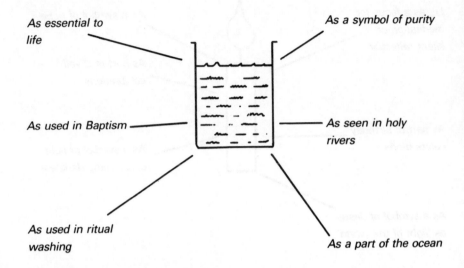

As essential to life

As a symbol of purity

As used in Baptism

As seen in holy rivers

As used in ritual washing

As a part of the ocean

Fig. 8.2 Example of an object used for collective worship

Such objects may not have any religious significance in themselves but can be used to illustrate religious themes. In this way everyday objects provide a focal point for the understanding of religious concepts.

People

In a previous chapter the value of using different people to present worship was described. Indeed, people provide one of the most effective resources in assembly. A mother bringing her new baby in, a Chinese father talking of his homeland, a charity worker describing her work, all present valuable opportunities for worthwhile learning.

Here are some further examples.

- Religious leaders (e.g. vicars, non-conformist ministers, rabbis, imams);
- Community leaders (e.g. representatives from religious groups);
- People from the community (e.g. nurse, elderly people, policeman);

- Charity organisers;
- Children (e.g. Brownies, Cubs, members of sports teams).

This last group must be treated with special sensitivity. In no way should a child be made to feel singled out as quaint or peculiar, and participation should be on a strictly voluntary basis. Many children who belong to groups such as the Brownies and Cubs may wear their uniform on special days. This presents an opportunity for them to explain their membership of such groups. I remember once, a boy coming to school in the new clothes he had been bought for Eid. He was delighted to show these off to the school and relate the events of the festival. Importantly, the teacher leading the assembly set a role model of respect, which was taken up by the children.

Support will often be needed for adults coming in to assembly. Teachers may need to lead the assembly, field questions and guide the visitor to appropriate subject matter. They will certainly be needed for discipline purposes and to introduce and thank the visitor.

A representative from a charitable organisation:

Fig. 8.3 Example of using a visitor in assembly

Using food in assembly

Food is a powerful symbol in religious traditions besides being an essential feature of human life. Because of this it can be a valuable resource for collective worship. Many festivals, celebrations and holy

92

days are accompanied by special food. Food laws and obligations are part of many traditions, as is the sharing of food during services. Collective worship, with its emphasis on coming together and sharing is an ideal time to explore the significance of food in religion.

It is a resource best saved for smaller group assemblies, and care should be taken not to include food which is forbidden to certain religious groups. Meat, for example, is best avoided altogether. Teachers should refer to books such as David Rose's *Home, School and Faith* (1992) for details about food laws.

Food in collective worship

From festivals e.g.	Mince pies	(Christian)
	Latkes	(Jewish)
	Sweets	(Hindu)
From worship e.g.	Matzot	(Jewish)
	Parshad	(Sikh)
From celebrations e.g.	Birthday cake	

Healthy food
From around the world
In the past
Sharing food
Preparing food
Being without food

A loaf of bread:

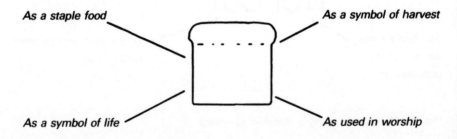

Fig. 8.4 Example of using food for collective worship

Audio-visual materials

Many schools now have the use of a number of AV resources. These will include radio, television, video, overhead projectors, cassette players and so on. Each one of these has a part to play in the presentation of worship.

There are television and radio programmes specifically designed for use in religious education and worship, e.g. *Together* (BBC Radio). However, there are other schools programmes which also offer stories or discussion points which can easily be used in assemblies e.g. *Our World* (Channel 4) and *You and Me* (BBC). Children's television programmes are also a valuable resource for worship, as many deal with issues which directly relate to children's lives. Programmes such as *Biker Grove*, *Grange Hill* and *Neighbours* (BBC) present dilemmas which affect children. Clips from such programmes can be the starting point for discussion, especially when teachers know that many of the children are regular viewers.

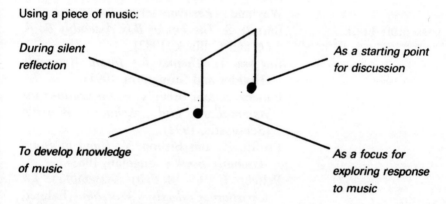

Using a piece of music:

During silent reflection

As a starting point for discussion

To develop knowledge of music

As a focus for exploring response to music

Fig. 8.5 Using AV materials for collective worship

Music can be an extremely effective resource in assembly, either as background as the children enter and leave or as the focal point of the worship. Music from a range of cultural traditions should be used and a collection might include pop, classical, traditional, folk music. Children should be encouraged to listen closely to music, whether it is presented live, on record and tape or on video.

Books for assemblies

Books will be an invaluable resource for worship and the following lists are separated into those for teachers' use and children's.

Teachers' books

Many books which give the legal framework for worship and guidance for practice are listed at the end of this book. The following list identifies those which will be of practical help in preparing assemblies.

World religions –	Cole, W. O. *Religion in the Multi-faith School* (Hulton, 1983).
	Cole, W. O. *Six Religions in the Twentieth Century* (Hulton, 1986).
	Hinnells, J. R. *Handbook of Living Religions* (Lion, 1983).
	Rose, D. *Home, School and Faith* (Fulton, 1992).
Festivals –	Macmillan – *Festivals* series.
	RMEP – *Living Festivals* series.
	Wayland – *Festivals* series.
Assembly books –	Barratt, S. *The Tinder Box Assembly Book* (A and C Black, 1982).
	Burgess, L. *Themes for Infant Assembly* (Hodder and Stoughton, 1991).
	Palmer, S. and Breuilly, E. *Inspirations for Assemblies and School Worship* (Scholastic, 1992).
	Proffit, R. and Bishop, V. *Hand in Hand Assembly Book* (Longman, 1983).
	Peirce, E. C. *Activity Assemblies for Christian Collective Worship* (Falmer, 1992).
	Peirce, E. C. *Activity Assemblies for Multi-racial Schools* (Falmer, 1992).
	Tillman, J. *Oxford Assembly Book* (Oxford University Press, 1989).
	Vause, D. and Beaumont, L. *The Junior Assembly Book* (Simon and Schuster Young Books, 1989).
	Wood, A. *Assembly Kit* (BBC Longman, 1991).
Biographies –	Hamish Hamilton – *Profiles* series.
	RMEP – *Faith in Action* series.
	SCM Press – *People with a Purpose* series.
	Wayland – *Great Lives* series.

Other publications–   CEM *Assembly File* (from the primary
                       mailing RE Today).
                       Scholastic Publications – Child Education.
                                                – Junior Education.
                                                – Art and Craft.

Children's books

Story books –   Ahlberg, A. *Please Mrs. Butler* (Puffin,
                       1983).
                       Briggs, R. *The Snowman* (Hamish
                       Hamilton, 1978).
                       Foreman, M. *War and Peas* (Picture
                       Puffin).
                       Hughes S. *Dogger* (Picture Lions, 1979).
                       Lewin, H. *Jafta's Family* series (Evans
                       Bros).
                       Tomlinson, J. *The Owl who was Afraid of
                       the Dark* (Puffin, 1983).
                       White, E. B. *Charlotte's Webb* (Hamish
                       Hamilton, 1981).
. . . and many others.
Stories from religions– Cole, W. O. *Religion in the Multi-faith
                       School* (Hulton, 1983).
                       Gavin, J. *Stories from the Hindu World*
                       (Macdonald, 1986). (Others in the series:
                       Jewish, Christian, Muslim, Sikh.)
                       Morgan, P. and Morgan, C. *Buddhist Stor-
                       ies* (Copyright, P. Morgan, Westminster
                       College, North Hinksey, Oxford, OX2
                       9AT).

Conclusion

We have seen how the possibilities for everyday resources for collective worship are endless and also how there is a wealth of material
specifically designed for assembly. Teachers appear to be constantly
looking for fresh ideas and new material. The demands of providing
worship every day puts a great strain on resources. However, if
teachers consider the variety of forms of worship, they will be able to
identify new ways of resourcing the activity without going to a great
deal of extra expense. Thinking creatively and widely about collective

96

worship will enable teachers to maximise the use of resources already around school to provide stimulating and effective assemblies.

CHAPTER 9
A Whole-school Approach to Collective Worship

Introduction

In recent years the value of developing a whole-school approach to curriculum and cross-curricular areas has been recognised. The development of whole-school policies which clearly set out the school's philosophies, aims and methods has been recognised as one way in which to improve provision. In most schools today, policy statements and their accompanying guidelines can be found for curriculum areas, special educational needs and issues which relate to interpersonal relationships, such as race, gender and discipline. Often, however, there is no written policy for collective worship. Of the three schools I studied (McCreery, 1991), none had clear guidelines for collective worship, and only one head teacher said they had anything approaching a statement for worship.

In this chapter the value of such a whole-school approach for worship is outlined. A framework for developing a whole-school approach will then be offered, including suggestions for ways forward and raising some of the issues which are likely to arise in forming a policy.

The value of whole-school planning

Traditionally the primary teacher's job has been an isolated and, to a great extent, an autonomous one. Closed classrooms and the absence of any national framework for primary education meant that what went on in the school was largely down to the individuals involved. In recent years, however, there has been a move to develop more collaborative ways of working. These have emerged for a variety of reasons. In a climate of increased accountability there has been pressure on teachers to publicise the work the children do, while sharing the content of their work has moved towards ensuring quality and effectiveness in the classroom. Changes in perceptions of management, with increased use of more collaborative approaches, has led to staff as a group taking more responsibility for the content of the curriculum, with post-holders consulting other staff in order to reach some consensus on what should be happening in school. Most recently, the demands of the National Curriculum have caused schools to review their provision and establish clear patterns so that all the subject areas can be covered sufficiently in the limited time available. It is now common to find whole-school themes which are set out afresh each year, and which staff come together to develop.

A whole-school approach to an area may take many forms. It usually involves senior management, post-holders and some or all of the staff, and may also include contributions from ancillary staff, governors, parents and pupils. The idea is that representatives from all groups involved in the life of the school contribute through discussion, meetings, questionnaires and so on to develop an agreed statement about the subject in hand. From here a framework for practice is developed which is available to all concerned. It is then used to inform day-to-day practice and as evidence available to governors, local authorities and inspectors. The best policies are those which are flexible enough to accommodate the styles of different personalities and minor changes in regulations when they arise. A crucial element in such policies is that they are dynamic: they are not written in tablets of stone for eternity, but are regularly reviewed and updated in the light of practice.

The value of such an approach to the development of provision in school is manifold. It offers members of the school community an opportunity to voice their opinions about a certain topic. When decisions are made collaboratively, there is more likely to be a feeling of ownership, which means that changes in policy and arrangements are more likely to succeed. There is also more likely to be a better sense of continuity, direction and progression in both subject and cross-curricular areas which gives the school stability and provides teachers with greater feelings of confidence and security. The development of a policy enables a school to identify its priorities and make clear its philosophy; clear goals are set which all members of the community are aware of. Such an approach can make explicit where the school is heading by reviewing current practice, establishing long-term goals and laying down clear criteria for material and human resourcing.

The process is not a speedy one, nor is it trouble free. The tensions of competing interests, personalities, limited budgets and so on, all make the process lengthy and often fraught, especially in areas which are contentious such as sex education. But the benefits can be worth the effort and can contribute to the effectiveness of the school.

The value of a whole-school approach for collective worship should be seen in the context of the above. Here is a controversial subject which is required by law and which touches the very deepest feelings of all members of the school community. It is an area which teachers may feel uncomfortable with, whether they be believers or not, and yet it is the one area in which there is little national guidance and only rather general help from local authorities. The head teacher is responsible for seeing that the law is followed, but she is given little help to identify either what worship should be for or what should be in it. In the absence of such guidance and because by law worship should reflect the character of the school, it is up to the school to define how it should be done.

While it is perfectly in order for the head teacher to decide on the form of worship for the school, it is clear, because of the controversial nature of school worship, that those who are to be involved in it should be consulted. In the three schools I worked with, it was clear that no discussion had taken place regarding worship. The head teachers appeared to have an understanding about their own image of worship, but staff and children tended to be confused and often concerned about what it was for and what it should contain. As a result, assemblies within each school showed a range of purpose, content and presentation which had little sense of cohesion, development of philosophy and in some cases were conflicting in aim. In one school, for example, it was a stated aim that assemblies should reflect the multi-cultural nature of the children, and yet the assemblies which were observed used only Christian prayers and hymns in which all the children were expected to join.

A whole-school policy for worship would allow those involved in the school to share their thoughts and opinions, to identify common ground and hopefully reach some kind of consensus on the purpose and presentation of worship. Collective worship should be seen as part of the children's religious education and as such needs a clear sense of structure and development. Goals need to be outlined, resources identified, outcomes established. Only in this way can a school be sure that it is treating collective worship as a valuable educational activity. Schools must also be able to justify their practice to parents, governors, the community and inspectors, and they therefore need to have a carefully thought-out policy which they are confident fulfils the law and makes assembly a worthwhile educational part of school life.

Developing a policy: points for consideration

There are many ways of beginning the process of developing a policy and schools will no doubt choose one which is appropriate to their situation. There are, however, some starting points which could form the basis of the endeavour.

The first thing to decide upon is who is to be involved. By law the head teacher is responsible for collective worship and it would seem essential that she is part of the process. How heads do this will be up to the individual: some may wish to take a back seat and act only as overseer, delegating the responsibility of organising the activity to others. If the school has an RE co-ordinator, this post-holder is likely to play a major role in the activity, as might other members of the management team. But the rest of the staff should also be involved in some way, even if they are not all going to be involved in leading assemblies, and representatives from the different age phases within the school should also be there, to ensure that the needs of the pupils are taken into account.

As well as the staff, other groups to be consulted should be the governors, parents and representatives of the local community, such as the leaders of the various faiths. The children too should be able to contribute to the discussion: a recognition of their perspective is obviously important if the policy is to succeed. Schools may also wish to make use of the expertise of RE specialists such as advisers and tutors involved in initial teacher education.

Secondly, starting points for discussion will revolve around the nature of the school and its community. A useful framework for getting planning off the ground can be found in the CEM publication, *Planning RE in Schools* (1991). Although this is intended for developing an RE policy and syllabus, it can easily be applied to collective worship. It identifies several factors for consideration when starting on a policy. These relate to the school, the staff, the children and the parents:

The school –	Is it in a rural, urban, inner-city area?
	Does it have links with the community?
	Does it have good relationships with parents?
The staff –	What are their faith, cultural, racial backgrounds?

Are they aware of the beliefs and practices of faith communities?

What is their knowledge, understanding of collective worship?

The children – What are the experiences of the children?

Are they used to working in the neighbourhood?

What levels of ability do they have?

The parents – What is known of their economic, cultural, religious backgrounds?

(See CEM, 1991, p2.)

To this list I would add five others:

- How would we describe the ethos of the school?
- What are our views on the nature of the curriculum?
- What policies are in place regarding equal opportunities?
- What attitudes towards worship are held by the staff?
- How do the children respond to assemblies in their present form?

The answers to these questions will mark the way forward for development. For example, if it becomes apparent that staff are not familiar with the terms of the 1988 Act, then some in-service work may be needed to develop their understanding. Similarly, information gained about families' religious backgrounds may help to identify those religious traditions which will form the basis of content. It may be found that some questions cannot be immediately answered. If this is the case then perhaps the school will need to spend time answering these first before it moves on.

A structure for the process needs to be outlined. A time scale might be set in place and responsibilities identified. What role will the different groups play in the process? Initial discussion needs to take place to agree on an agenda but part of the process will need to involve small group discussion, reporting back, larger group discussion and so on. The CEM booklet (1991) recommends that initial discussions should take place in groups of two, three or four people, a spokesperson from which reports back to larger meetings. Suggestions for the organisation of the process is given in the sections which follow.

Initial data collection

1. The co-ordinator reviews present provision – frequency of assembly, times, content and materials used etc. Ideas from the pupils could be included (see next section).

2. The main points emerging from small group discussion based on factors outlined above, are documented and distributed.
3. The points identified under 2 are then addressed at larger meetings.

The role which pupils might play

In my study of three schools, pupils expressed a variety of opinions about assemblies. Some of these views were positive, some negative, but it was clear that because of the regular nature of assembly, children recognised it as an established feature of school life. The children were able to explain why they enjoyed some assemblies and not others, and were able to identify what they thought the purpose of the activity was. Such information would be valuable in developing a policy on worship. Ways of tapping the children's thoughts might include such ideas as:

- getting the pupils to write/talk/draw about the assemblies they have valued the most and least;
- a simple questionnaire, the responses to which a group of pupils collate and present to the co-ordinator;
- giving pupils the opportunity to make suggestions for changes and new kinds of assembly.

Resolutions

From large group discussion, it may be necessary to draw up a list of certain problems to be addressed. For instance, in schools where pupils are predominantly from non-Christian faiths, the school may feel it appropriate to apply to the SACRE (Standing Advisory Council on Religious Education) for exemption from Christian worship. An example of the procedure for this is given in the guidelines for worship from Wandsworth SACRE (1990). It begins with the head teacher consulting the governors, who should in turn consult parents. The case is considered by the SACRE based on the evidence put forward by the head teacher. The SACRE makes a decision in consultation with the adviser for religious education who represents the director of education. A decision is made on a majority basis and the SACRE can vote to accept or reject without modification. The decision is then communicated to the head teacher stating the date from which the determination takes effect. The responsibility is then with the head to decide what form the alternative worship should take. The decision is reviewed after five years.

The majority of schools, however, may find it unnecessary to apply to the SACRE for a determination. Their interpretation of the Act may allow for a varied approach to worship which can encompass all the faiths which are represented in the school. Once that decision is made, priorities need to be identified and a long-term plan initiated. Such long-term plans could usefully be related to six different aspects of collective worship:

- organisation e.g. grouping, venues, times of day;
- interpreting 'collective worship' e.g. understanding the terms of the Act;
- content and presentation;
- resources;
- evaluation;
- withdrawals (of both children and staff).

An excellent summary of the various questions a school might need to ask in developing their policy is outlined in *School Worship* by Bill Gent (1989). These 25 questions cover both practical and theoretical aspects of assembly, for example:

- How many staff contribute to assemblies?
- How far ahead are assemblies planned?
- Are appropriate ideas about religion being perpetuated?
- Is there too much moralising?

(See Gent, 1989, p17.)

Drafting a policy statement

One of the first priorities to work towards will be the drafting of a statement which sets out the school's intentions for collective worship. This should make clear how the school sees worship in terms of purpose and value. It should also be available for any interested groups to examine, such as governors, SACRE and parents, and should be written in terms which are accessible for people who are not closely involved in educational practice. A policy statement would need to include the following:

- some reference to the 1988 Act upon which the policy is based;
- some reference to any LEA guidelines;
- a statement regarding the ethos and values of the school upon which the worship policy is to be based;
- a statement of the value and purpose of worship within the school;

- a brief outline of what such worship might contain;
- a reference to the withdrawal clauses available to parents and teachers.

An example of a draft policy statement for collective worship

* Collective worship in our school is based upon the terms of the 1988 Education Reform Act which states that:
  - collective worship should be provided each day for all pupils;
  - the majority of acts of worship in a term should be broadly Christian, reflecting broad traditions of Christian belief;
  - collective worship should be appropriate having regard to the family backgrounds, ages and aptitudes of the pupils involved.

* Collective worship in our school is seen as part of religious education and is also based on the values and qualities which we consider important, such as:
  - respect for every individual;
  - respect for our environment;
  - enabling every member of our school to achieve their potential.

* The purpose of collective worship in our school is to:
  - reflect on significant features of human life;
  - explore our response to the world we live in;
  - learn about the traditions of the different religions represented in our school;
  - learn about the Christian traditions upon which our society is based;
  - enable us to develop our own response to the spiritual side of life.

* Children will not be required to participate in activities which are contrary to the beliefs of their family.
* They will be encouraged to respond positively to the religious experiences of humankind.
* The law allows parents to withdraw their children from collective worship. Teachers are also allowed to withdraw from collective worship. It is hoped, however, that worship in our school is of a kind which includes everyone.

The statement should then be open to discussion by all parties involved in the process. Once finalised it can be included in school prospectuses so that it is easily available for interested parties to read.

Developing the statement into long-term plans

The establishment of a general policy is only one step along the route to effective worship. Specific long-term plans need to follow to identify the needs of the school and prioritise them. Such plans will emerge from a consideration of the practical aspects of collective worship. Schools might wish to address questions such as those listed below:

- How will we group children for worship?
- Who will lead the worship?
- How will it be resourced?
- What methods of presentation will we use?
- What materials will we use?
- What links will be drawn with the curriculum?
- How can we ensure that children are active participants?
- What do we do about the children whose parents ask that they do not attend?
- Will we plan for assembly across a year, a term, a week?
- How do we evaluate collective worship? (See next section.)

Consideration of these questions will help to identify any INSET needs among the staff and help to identify resource requirements. Individuals may be identified to take responsibility for different tasks. Once needs are prioritised, a time schedule can be set for the introduction of new practices. The time allowed for development should be realistic, but it should also be reviewed regularly to check progress.

Evaluation

This is an essential part of the long-term planning. There are two aspects to evaluation. First there is an evaluation of the success of the process of reviewing and developing worship. This may be carried out during each step of the process as well as at the end when the policy is in place. There will need to be a time identified for this terminal evaluation when revisions may need to be made.

The other aspect of evaluation is that which applies to the assemblies themselves. How should a subject like collective worship be evaluated? Should it be based upon the achievement of the children or perhaps more realistically, the quality of their response?

The concept of curriculum evaluation is common to primary schools and serves to ensure effective schooling. In collective worship the concept is more recent and perhaps more problematic, but it still needs to play a part. Evaluating assemblies can serve a variety of purposes. Firstly it ensures that collective worship is taking place and that it fulfils the requirements of the law. Secondly it enables the head and staff to monitor the content of assembly within the school thus ensuring a variety of subject matter and presentation. Thirdly, it promotes effective assemblies and ensures that they are fulfilling an educational purpose and not simply a matter of form.

Although collective worship is distinct from religious education, guidelines provided for RE by local authorities can be useful. In recent Agreed Syllabuses, the question of assessment has been addressed. It is recognised that this venture is not without its problems, but equally, the importance of monitoring pupils' progress in all aspects of the curriculum is recognised as a feature of current educational practice. Agreed Syllabuses tend to begin by expressing reservations about assessment in RE. For example, the Cornwall (1989) syllabus states:

> Religious Education occurs in a variety of ways in school, not only in the structured lessons within the curriculum, but also in the ethos, rules, and general tone of the school. Evaluation of Religious Education in all these areas is clearly very difficult because of the different values which people hold, and because there are no agreed criteria by which to assess. (p22)

A further reservation expressed, is one which relates not only to RE but to many other aspects of school life:

> In addition, like much else in education, Religious Education is essentially preparation for adult life, therefore it cannot be fully evaluated whilst the pupil is still in school. (p22)

Whilst assessment in education is clearly a significant feature, and will be so for the foreseeable future, it must be remembered that the form which it takes is by no means universally agreed. We must avoid necessarily trying to fit RE and in particular, collective worship, into the same kind of framework as other curriculum areas, for this may not be appropriate. It is certainly possible to assess what knowledge the children have gained as a result of assemblies, but the concept of measuring 'spiritual development' is more elusive. Many writers are agreed that the idea of establishing levels of development in areas such as attitudes, spirituality, beliefs, is not desirable, even if consensus could be achieved on criteria for assessment. For example, the CEM publication, *Planning RE in Schools* (1991), recognises some of the limitations on assessing children's learning in RE:

It should be recognised, though, that despite all the care that can be taken to devise or select suitable methods, what is evaluated will cover a narrower range than the total set of aims. (p41)

The writers of the Culham Report (1992) found that many schools were resisting the temptation to treat RE like the other curriculum areas as far as assessment was concerned. One respondent commented: 'Generally we do not believe NC (National Curriculum) terminology/assessment etc. necessary to improve the quality of RE' (p21).

Although collective worship is not easy to evaluate, schools have found that the keeping of records on assembly helps to ensure quality and provide information for periodic reviews of their success. The record begins with perhaps a termly plan of assemblies, then daily records are kept of each assembly, identifying the leader, the theme, the content etc. An example is given below.

DATE	Mon. 6th June
LEADER	Ms Smith
GROUP	All year 1/2
THEME	Loneliness
AIMS/PURPOSE	To help children develop empathy with those who are lonely
PRESENTATION METHODS	Picture of lonely child/story telling
RESOURCES	*Smith the Lonely Hedgehog*, Althea (Dinosaur Publications)
EVALUATION	The children listened attentively to the story and answered questions about what it feels like to be lonely, with sensitivity.
COMMENTS MADE BY VISITORS	Some parents who attended said they thought the assembly set a very positive attitude to the subject.
FUTURE DEVELOPMENT?	A story about a person who was lonely?

Records such as these enable schools to answer questions about the value and effectiveness of their assemblies. Such questions might be:

- Are the assemblies a valuable educational experience?
- Do the children enjoy them? Have they been responsive?
- Have assemblies suited all age groups and children of different attainments?

- Do they fulfil the terms of the 1988 Act?
- Are there links with the rest of the curriculum?
- Which kinds of assembly seem to have been best received?
- Are individual's beliefs respected?
- Have parents and other visitors valued the assemblies?

Such consideration of the children's learning in assembly time will help to maintain high-quality activities which allow for progression and development within collective worship.

Conclusion

The central purpose of this chapter has been to show how a systematic approach to the development of collective worship in the primary school can serve to improve and sustain the quality of provision. There may be much work to be done in planning a policy, and worship may have to compete with demands from the rest of the curriculum, but the value of such an endeavour will be great and long lasting. A central theme in the development of a whole-school policy is openness, whereby each group within the school can feel free to contribute, whatever their personal beliefs. Of course there may be some who do not wish to be involved because of their own views and they should not feel pressurised to do so. There will be need for a good deal of compromise, especially where individuals are arguing from opposite extremes: such compromise should not be seen as failure, but as an area which may need to be re-addressed at a later date. Another aspect essential to the development of effective assemblies is the use made of evaluation. This needs to be a feature of both long-term planning and each assembly.

Once a policy is in place, this does not mean the task of planning is completed. Regular reviews will be needed to update it in the light of new circumstances and evaluation. It should be remembered that a policy is only effective as long as it is being implemented and plays an active part in day-to-day planning and practice. It relies for its success on the interest, enthusiasm and commitment of those who are working within it.

Bibliography

Alexander, R., Rose, J. and Woodhead, C. (1992) *Curriculum Organisation and Classroom Practice in Primary Schools. A Discussion Paper*. London: DES.

Althea (1983) *Smith the Lonely Hedgehog*. London: Dinosaur Publications.

Bastide, D. (1987) *Religious Education 5–12*. Lewes: Falmer Press.

Bastide, D. (1992) *Good Practice in Primary Religious Education 4–11*. Lewes: Falmer Press.

British Council of Churches (1989) *Worship in Education*. London: British Council of Churches.

CEM (Christian Education Movement) (1991) *Planning RE in Schools*. Middlesex: CEM Publications.

CEM (Christian Education Movement) (1992) *Worship File*. Middlesex: CEM Publications.

Copley, T. (1989) *Worship, Winners and Worries*. National Society/Church House Publishing.

Cornwall Education Committee (1989) *Syllabus for Religious Education*. Cornwall County Council.

Cox, E. (1983) *Problems and Possibilities for Religious Education*. London: Hodder & Stoughton Educational.

Cox, E. and Cairns, J. (1989) *Reforming Religious Education*. London: Kogan Page.

Culham College Institute (1992) *Religious Education and Collective Worship in Primary Schools*. Culham College Institute.

DES (Department of Education and Science) (1989) *Religious Education and Collective Worship* (Circular 3/89). London: HMSO.

Durham Report (1970) *The Fourth R*. London: SPCK.

Gent, B. (1989) *School Worship: Perspectives, Principles and Practice*. Middlesex: CEM Pubications.

Goldman, R. (1965) *Readiness for Religion.* London: Routledge and Kegan Paul.

Goldman, R. (1964) *Religious Thinking from Childhood to Adolescence.* London: Routledge and Kegan Paul.

Hansard (1988) *Official report of parliamentary debates,* 12th and 16th May.

Hay, D. (1987) *Exploring Inner Space.* London: Mowbery.

Holm, J. (1975) *Teaching Religion in School.* London: Oxford University Press.

Hughes, S. (1979) *Dogger.* London: Picture Lions.

Hull, J. (1975) *School Worship: An Obituary.* London: SCM Press.

Hull, J. (1989a) *The Act Unpacked: The Meaning of the 1988 Education Act for Religious Education.* University of Birmingham and CEM.

Hull, J. (1989b) 'Editorial' in *British Journal of Religious Education* Vol. 11.

Hull, J. (1990) 'Editorial' in *British Journal of Religious Education* Vol. 12.

Hull, J. (1991) 'Editorial' in *British Journal of Religious Education* Vol. 13.

McCreery, E. (1991) *An Investigation into the Effects of the 1988 Education Reform Act on Collective Worship in Primary Schools.* Unpublished M.A. dissertation, Roehampton Institute, University of Surrey.

Mumford, C. (1982) *Young Children and Religion.* London: Edward Arnold.

National Curriculum Council (1991) *Analysis of SACRE Reports 1991.* York: NCC.

National Curriculum Council (1992) *Analysis of SACRE Reports 1992.* York: NCC.

Palmer, S. and Breuilly, E. (1992) *Inspirations for Assembly and School Worship.* Leamington Spa: Scholastic Publications Ltd.

Peirce, E. (1991) *Activity Assemblies for Christian Collective Worship.* Lewes: Falmer Press.

Peirce, E. (1992) *Activity Assemblies for Multi-racial Schools.* Lewes: Falmer Press.

Proffitt, R. and Bishop, V. (1983) *Hand in Hand Assembly Book.* London: Longman Group Ltd.

Rose, D. (1992) *Home, School and Faith.* London: David Fulton Publishers.

Slee, N. (1989) *The Question of School Worship.* Unpublished notes, Roehampton Institute.

Slee, N. (1990) 'Developments in School Worship: An Overview' in *Journal of Beliefs and Values* Vol. 11.

Souper, P. C. and Kay, W. K. (1982) *The School Assembly Debate: 1942–1982.* University of Southampton.

Sullivan, D. (1990) *R.E. The Primary Years.* London: Collins.

Tilby, A. (1979) *Teaching God.* London: Fontana.

Wandsworth SACRE (1990) *Guidelines for Collective Worship in*

Wandsworth Schools. Wandsworth LEA.

Warwickshire County Council (1990) *A Time to Share. A Practical Guide to Worship in Warwickshire Schools.* Warwickshire County Council.

Webster, J. (1990) 'School Worship' in *British Journal of Religious Education* Vol. 13.

White, J. (1989) 'A Humanist Response' in Cox, E. and Cairns, J. *Reforming Religious Education.* London: Kogan Page.

Index